# SUGARFREE MAILB@X

selected poems of

UMAPADA KAR

translated by

Swapan Roy

Alok Biswas

Aryanil Mukherjee

Runa Bandyopadhyay

Kaushik Chakrabarty

Bhaswati Goswami

Manik Saha

Nilima Deb

Debadrita Bose

&

Umapada Kar

flying turtle

Sugarfree Mailbox

A Collection of Poems by Umapada Kar

ISBN 978-93-89953-43-5

First Edition - 2022

Published by Flying Turtle, an imprint of

Sristisukh Prokashan LLP, Bagnan, Howrah - 711312

Cover - Debashish Saha



Price: INR 249 / USD 14.99

Printed by Sristisukh Print (www.sristisukhprint.com)

Outlet - 72/2a Potuatola Lane, Kolkata 9

Contact - 9910270432, 7829741797

Dedicated

to

All the Translators

(except myself)

# Few Words

Ideally, a poet should not have any forewords in his own collection of Poems. His poems are his representative. Poetry itself can identify him, justify his words, and can express his unexpressed items. Poetry is the parameter of his thinking, consciousness, feelings, and uprightness. Still, a few words are necessary here for me to emphasize the characteristics of this book.

Since this book is a selection from several individual collections published over a wide time span, no one can get a single taste from it. On the contrary, they will get different tastes, observations, and makings, with different ups and downs of that phase of time. It was a tuff task for me to select the poems from thirteen books keeping in mind that all remaining others are also my creations, my makings. It was a challenge for me, and I don't know whether it has been done correctly or not. Again it is a collection, where the poems originally written in Bengali have been translated to English. Here also some differences exist in this collection. In general, it is observed that a single translator has done this type of job. But in this collection ten translators including myself have been engaged for the job. As all they are poets, the sensation and style of translation or transcreation are different. Readers may get different tastes and making mechanisms and angles also. In fact, it is a new type of project work.

In my opinion, poetry exists always everywhere from small insects to wide open sky. A poetry-writer being driven or triggered holds the shapeless body-less poetry in the brain through his observations, hearings, and interactions with inert and living, in a different angle of looking and thinking, which generally can't. After germination through digestion and reduction, the poetry writer can write in letters, words, and sounds only a little of his feelings and thinking. The source-poetry remains in his head (brain) intact. As a result, we may say that thinking is poetry, which is mostly an incomplete expression of the writer's feelings, consciousness, and source consideration. Now it's a process to write down. So many words and expressions appear from the signals of the brain, and a poetry writer starts to think about what should be written and what shouldn't. It is the job of a poet to go through negation and negation and also with filtration.

I do also think that era of sub-consciousness is over. Making of poetry must be a conscious effort. We know about three stages of consciousness. But another stage of consciousness, called expansive consciousness, can nourish a pivotal role from the very beginning of the poetry to its end. It is also a thought process to arrive at this stage of consciousness and keep one to remain in this stage. Not only changes outside of poetry are observed, but also it can change the inner soul of the poetry. With this spirit poet writes his original poetry without copying, remixing, or remaking the old one. Here it is so much acute and sharp that the necessity of orientation of the subject, storytelling, essay writing, special massage giving, or preserving memorable speech through poetry become invalid. Even the metaphor, simile, ornate language, the art of rhetoric, poetical meter, and the old tools of verse can be avoided for new poetry. The directive force for writing poetry will be the expansive consciousness, as a result, the poetry will be open-ended, limitless, without any rock logic, not linear but multi-dimensional, centrifugal, or without any single center, may have so many centers, subject and object may replace themselves, only possibilities are real. Truth doesn't exist at all. We make truth every now and then, which is apparent. Last-day's truth replaces itself with Today's truth, and Today's also by Tomorrow's one. Still, poets try to reach and remain nearer to the apparent truth.

Poetry is an endless journey from one void to another void, and the journey is colorful, with its ups and downs; through its friction, action, and interaction with living and non-living beings, especially human beings; with the coexistence of the cosmos and obviously nature, the material world as a whole. The creator of poetry doesn't satisfy with his single first-life living, a second life-living that is full of possibilities and dreams and runs parallel to that first one. All these thinking are for the search for a new type of poetry, and for getting a release or free access from conventional poetry writing.

All these efforts from all corners may feel well if the work touches and impresses the different readers of international language English.

With thanks and love.

Umapada Kar

Kolkata

# Expansive Consciousness, Contra Transcendence: A Dialogue with Umapada Kar's *Sugarfree Mailbox*

I.

Mixing shadow with light this is Derjeeling and Dooars.

A day with tea color
...
uttered so long ago...

("A Child of Light and Darkness,"
*Sugarfree Mailbox*)

Tea infused with shadow and light (a light belonging to darkness) seeps, as color, into the day. This is my first encounter with the poem of expansive consciousness, alight belonging to the very core of darkness.

The passage reminds me of lines by the Turkish poet

Orhan Veli:

*How beautiful the color of tea*
*Is*
*In the morning*
*In the fresh air.*
*How beautiful*
*The fresh air*
*is.*
*How beautiful the young boy*
*Is.*
*How beautiful the tea*
*is.*[1]

In both, there is an act from the core of the poet's being (his/her soul) to the outside world seeking a union between the poet's consciousness and the "waves," tantra of the world. This is the new real, this day with tea *color: simple*, saturated with a spiritual light; simultaneously, *elusive*, existing in the darkness of the poem.

Where does this centrifugal synthesis occur— more precisely, where does Umapada Kar locate it?

The rest of "A Child of Light and Darkness," written in 2017, deals with the opposing tension between the crying child (the child in all of us) and the darkness outside (the "whining rain") that in another poem[2], pouring non-stop for five days in monsoon, loses its temporal identity and is altered into a pure number— revealing a shadowy core, which is light!, within itself, "the Fifth is its identity/...I show its blackish face". The poem deals with the poet's endless struggle to fuse the consciousness of the vulnerable child and the forces surrounding it into a *fluid* space, a *new real* where multiple realities, "making face with another and the other," coexist:

...

*But what shall I do with this presentation!*
*If the child continues to cry and the whining rain*
*wants to suppress the mouth of the child again and*
*again*
*Is it any indicator for the conversion of the lighted day to*
*darkness?*
*For which no meter has yet been invented to measure*
*What shall I do with this light mixed with shadow?*
*How can I satisfy my taste of tea, if the child of Derjeeling*
*doesn't play together with the child of Dooars!*
*If one makes face with another and the other*
*doesn't burst out with laughter!*

("A Child of Light and Darkness,"
translated by Umapada Kar)

Here again, I am reminded of lines by another Turkish poet, Cemal Süreya: the same urge to join the cosmic with the child-like in the joyful realty of a child's game, "the whining rain" in cahoots in the process:

*the stars were on the sidewalk*
*as if at the prophet's coming*
*because it had drizzled the night before*
*dizzy like a cloud, i left the house*
*skipping, skipping on the stars*
*pleased as punch in the moonlight*
*playing hopscotch*
*as at the prophet's coming*
*because it had drizzled the night before*

(Cemal Süreya, Animals of Dawn[3] )

## II.

Where is the centrifugal center of consciousness in Umapada's poetry from which the images expand? It is the speaker's home, its rising and descending stairs, his living room, his curtains, his broken piano, the bathroom mirror (in front of which his clownish figure with false teeth stands holding a toothbrush), etc. etc.; in other words, it is the *space* where is housed the intimate frailty of his being, his desires. Here lies Umapada's drastic step as a poet: the classical static location of consciousness (the pronoun "I") is shifted to a dynamic space where, split, multiple aspects of consciousness (projected on "objects") can interact with each other in tangential *unreal* reflections. These reflections constitute the light of the poem.... And can interact with the forces outside the home on the other side of the "sugarfree mailbox" (*water-stair/stair-case*). The poet Runa Bandyopadhyay expresses this quality of Umapada's poetry succinctly:

> *His magnificent and multidimensional poems objectify an object to refer its properties with a centrifugal journey by decentralizing consciousness. His poems create an imaginary space with the refracted light of his own experiences.*

*A mosquito-curtain has hanged itself without any hook.*
("Jokes and Magic"[4])

*The eyes of mine open.*
*as drops of you*
*fall upon me*
*With those eyes*
*I see you whole*
*in the fragments.*

("Ma, opens up the details"[5])

*scattered your hair*
*on what doesn't occur*
*dropped a mass of darkness at the entrance*
*to the underworld...*
*standing with lips wide open at its front door...*

("Earns on Beggary: 24"[6])

Doors, windows separate this dynamic core from "the other", that includes garden creatures, the wind, the birds, the moon (its shadowy light), stars, the river; but most crucially the rain (you, the lover) that enacting its blessing in a relentless downpour darkens. Umapada's poetry of the *unreal real* is developed out of the interweaving interactions of these two polarities. The outside (the other) constantly penetrates the home; the consciousness, simultaneously, extends, expands to meet it. In the poems' lines both the outer and inner break down, losing their autonomy; reappearing in *unified* molecular *re-arrangements* where fragments from both re-appear like shining atoms, projecting the most intense light, "with those eyes/I see the whole/in fragments".

The "sugarfree mailbox" is the emblem of the porous skin (the metaphysical threshold) through which, in both directions, the deconstructive interweaving occurs:

*Chameleon pulls its hand back after*
*touching lightly.*
*Warp of sari is in metamorphoses colour,*
*weaving out flying butterfly...*

("Untitled – 3"[7], 2017)

*Let the snail be light in its shell*
*Let the mighty stars originate in our stretched*
*dark hair Cluster of rays born from every pore of*
*our skin.*

("Away from Few Light Years"[8])

*The moon goes below poverty line in the depths of the night. Shredding a few buffalo-clouds it swells in country liquor. In the darkness of zero kerosene, a snatch of butter moonlight makes the woodman sex up...*

("Prow filling me"[9])

*The evening candles' singing-anklets not again*
*known to the mirror.*

("Earns on Beggary:16"[10])

(Only the light of a "mass of darkness" belongs to the mirror.)

*Bubbling*

*When I turn a water page, poems float up. And lost somewhere with small waves of water. It continues until my own grows within me.*

*As the kite-spool opens its thread, poems start flying. Its tremulous wave in random wind remains unclear. As long as I shake myself by shouting hurrah.*

*The flying dove of interior can't be understood from exterior. Few drops of rain from cloud make the poetry-bird to fly by overcoming its inertia. Set the sail with mastto sail through river.*

*Negation becomes wet and lustre scatters by crossing*

*the hazy light. A ringing tone synchronizes with my dizzy brain. All my dryness become aqueous lowland.*

("Bubbling"[11])

*Finally imagination self-referred*
*Blowing away black soot from the dwindling woke*
*Sits humming in front of a clean oven*
*Throw-in-some- grain faith cooks to soft floral rice*

("M"[12])

**

While *the do/or* and the *wind/ows* open the consciousness to the reality of the monsoon, the sailboat in the river, the bird, etc. – *the mirr/or* (fronted by medicine bottles and the clownish toothless figure), the *dwindling/wok*, the sparkles from the *crema/torium*[13]" and the *graph/ sheet* (against which a spring-wind-up-doll is leaning) open consciousness (and poetry) to a mass of darkness, a tabula rasa of infinite, with no end, on which *language/ and consciousness* must imprint itself. They create the parallel spaces in Apadana's poetry:

...

*The floor of the stage*
*A white paper.*

("The Galaxy and Thinking"[14])

*Bell and silence oscillating alongside. Ding-dong and its resonance... and the next.. My ears advancing with small steps into its labyrinth.*

("Cosmic Bell"[15])

*Doll – 2.*

*A spring-wind-up doll*
*Has been seated before a graph sheet*
*The doll plays a drum automatically with the*
*winds*

*Each square of the graph sheet*
*Is overflowing with atoms of sound*
*When the music stops*
*A violin could be spotted behind*
*But the bow is missing*
*As the sketch remained incomplete*
*For want of winds in the spring*

III.

*Sugarfree Mailbox* covers selections from Umapada's poetry from 1979 to 2017. From the earliest poems to the very last, a self-mocking humor and rich humanity, filled with the furniture and activities of every day life, permeate his work – lozenges, homeopathic medicine bottles, ceiling fans, mosquito nets, etc, etc. Simultaneously, the "bell of silence", so prominent in the late work, is already here in the shadows, in the very structure of the images. To this poet, the following lovely lines from the early work give a funny, filmic picture of social customs and interactions inside a Bengali home. Nevertheless, the basic elements of the later more philosophical poetry – the interactions between outside and inside, the penetration of *there* into the room — is already present, here, in the room, as the messengers of an alternate transformed space:

*Just few minutes; if you come, you have to sit down;*

*that's our custom.*
*Even if you don't sit, water, tea and biscuits come.*
*And if you sit in cross-legged position, mosquitos,*
*ants, white lizard come.*

("Drawing Room"[17])

Umapada's intimate, witty, self-effacing humanity – resonant with a melancholy (or sweet sadness) emanating from a mysterious place — is why his lines consistently remind me of Orhan Veli:

*When train windows sleep.*
*Boats from rivers climb up eyes.*

("The leftover vessel and shelter"[18])

*The Sea*

*I, in my room overlooking the seashore,*
*Not looking out of the window,*
*Know that the boats sailing out in the sea*
*Go loaded with watermelons.*[19]

*Inside*

*Windows are better;*
*At least you see the birds passing by*
*Instead of four walls.*[20]

## IV.

I first met Umapada in February, 2019, at an impromptu gathering around a coffee house table in Kolkata, made possible by Runa Bandyopadhyay, of a number of poets associated with the school of Expansive Consciousness in Bengali (among them Umapada Kar, Swapam Roy, Runa Bandyopadhyay, Pranab Pal and Atanu Bandyopadhyay) and three American poets (Elizabeth Willis, Adeena Karasick and myself) who were in Kolkata for the Book Fair to celebrate the publication of the special issue on American Poetry *Bridgeable Lines*, edited by Runa Bandyopadhyay and Aritra Sanyal. It was a significant, revealing, delightful event, for me the high point of our visit in Kolkata that year, that lasted over two hours where Bengali and American poets had a chance to talk to each other, hear each others' works.

During the gathering, in English translation, Umapada read an elusive, philosophical text by Barin Ghosal at the root of which the text seemed to propose a poetics of *the unreal, the reality of the non-existent*. The idea perked my interest immediately because I was proposing and exploring a similar idea in my most recent poem at the time *Animals of Dawn* the entirety of which I had read in Kolkata two years before. I turned to Runa, who was sitting next to me and had translated passages from *Animals of Dawn* into Bengali, giving her a knowing look, suggesting that now I realized how my poetry spoke to her and her poet friends so directly and viscerally:

*Non-existent, still the 2 BHK flat seems to be there*

*Two floating buoys inside, still I think, they aren't*
*Yet drifting, with what a magic?*

*I am inside the room, obsessed, the two rooms seem*
*to be limitless*

*It seems a little opening will never end*

("Untitled - 6"[22] )

*Dracula*

*"Horatio: I'll cross it, though it blast me. Stay, illusion!*
*Speak to me..."*

*Existence is a very rare event,*
*out of the infinities that don't happen.*
*These lines're about the left out.*

*And their liberation.*
*The non-existent, you have nothing to lose*
*but your walls!*

"Two floating buoys," inside the speaker's room, full of the everyday objects of daily life – opening, through "a little opening" in the wall, to a "limitless" room. The two spaces inside/outside each other, simultaneous. Floating centers of an ellipse, endlessly *there, here.* The all-encompassing space of expanding consciousness.

## V.

The (Non-)Existing

The two buoys in Umapada's poetry are in the same space.

The transcendent (centrifugal expansion) involves a departure which is also an arrival (there is here). The actual and imagined are on an equal footing, both real; in fact the silent cosmic bell of only-imagined — not actually happened — more powerful because infinite. The light from a "few light years" away is the light of consciousness itself, its centrifugal realness:

*Bell and silence oscillating alongside. Ding-dong*
*and its*
*resonance... and the next.. My ears advancing with*
*small steps*
*into its labyrinth.*

("Cosmic Bell"[23] )

Bell and silence, the two sides of the quantum screen. Umapada's lines/his floating rooms ring the cosmic bell.

The concept of the "non-existent" in the West is often entangled with the idea of the transcendent and framed as part of a duality: as opposed to "existent" or between true or false, logical and nonsensical, body and soul; in language (implicitly in poetry) it is between signifier (concrete word, its sound or noise) and signified (ephemeral and elusive). The relationship between the two is static, *no jump from one to the other possible.* Descartes calls the human body a machine and the soul the ghost in the machine. In the 17th century, the proper activity of mankind becomes exploring the machine through "observable" facts or "beautiful" mathematical theorems — and the dynamic "scientific" correspondence between the two. For all purposes, mathematical rigor replaces the soul as legitimate subject of endeavor. The soul is called inscrutable, untalkable, at best, *only* the language of religion. In other words, Descartes deprives the soul of speech.

His philosophy steals mathematics from the language of the soul (which was historically always a treasure house of images for it) and gives it to the body-machine. All this happens because of the radical discovery that if one treats the physical body (and the world) as a machine and weds it to mathematics, one becomes the king and master of nature's empire.

That is why Umapada's self-abnegating humor and modesty, his "toothless" expression of vulnerability in the face of the unknown is so crucial in his poetry.

"Techne" implied "making art" in Greece in its etymological origins. Descartes re-conceives the meaning of the word into "technology," making machines.

New Poetry, the poetics of expansive consciousness, attacks the static, unbridgeable separation of this duality in the West. In that respect, it is a radical rejection of a basic conceptual framework. That is its significance: opening a new avenue of thought, therefore, of language. In this poetry knowledge is created (i.e. *exists*) by a wedding between the mind and pin-points in the universe — *and is devoid of any element of power or control.* What consciousness doesn't touch is unknown. Since what is unknown is infinitely more than what is known, a sense of modesty and suffering, *a spiritual weakness - as a melody of the have-not-* is essential to this poetry — what Turkish calls *hüzün* (radical melancholy). That is why I am so attracted to the sweet vulnerability and humor of Umapada's lines; and why his work reminds me so of Orhan Veli whose humorous lines also are permeated with a mysterious sadness, never spelled but always there, expressed in the barest, simplest "sugarfree" language.

*

The *Eda* poetics I developed preparing *Eda: An*

*Anthology of Contemporary Turkish Poetry* and then applied to my American poems in English from *The Spiritual Life of Replicants* depicts the evolving processes of thought (consciousness) as they move and change, prior to being fixed (i.e. *happened*) into categorical, hierarchical thought structures. It embodies the "tissue of thought in motion", fluid, feminine, pre-existent, *only* imagined. It is a poetry of the have-not (of the 99%), infused with "melancholy." When the *Eda* anthology came out in 2004, my dear friend Aryanil Mukherjee wrote me how *Eda* could also be the poetics of Bengali poetry. He translated and interviewed Turkish poets and wrote about *Edain* Bengali publications. Though I believed him, I did not know what he meant until, for me, the ground-breaking meeting in the coffee house in 2019. I am eternally grateful and would like to thank Aryanil for seeing our stunning spiritual connection then and creating the original impetus for our wonderful collaborations fifteen years later.

In a case of wondrous quantum coherence, starting in the late 1880's, all these years I wrote my poetry, translations and essays with no knowledge of what was happening, simultaneously, in a different continent[25]:

*The concept of Expansive Consciousness suggests the expansion from the centre of the consciousness towards the surface of the waves, and if it moves forward consciously, then the continuous changes of unknown positions will allow the consciousness to expand. (Barin Ghosal)*

*Mayflies*[26]

*Infinite possibility doesn't mean freedom, but that it*
*may happen infinitely*

*but of maybes*

*Infinite possibility, within finality*

*that is the pharos rhythm perception of freedom*
*as gestures of maybes*

*prr*

*object ivities in a mirror existing*

*in continuum.*

VI.

I want to end this essay — more a dialogue between Umapada's poems and my work and the space surrounding both of us — by simply juxtaposing four texts. Reading Umapada's lines, I sensed a deep connection between the concept of *arcs of ascent and descent* in *Eda* and New Poetry of expansive consciousness; and an equally strong connection between the importance of home and its immediate surrounding area (balcony, garden, mailbox, river, etc.) and their importance in my recent poems:

*In its pre-Islamic origins, Sufism unifies contradictions, more precisely, perceives, intuits experience before its splits into opposites. The Islam introduces a mathematical language into this intuition. God, the lover, and the human lover are one, turning to and into each other, through a process both violent and loving.*

*Arcs of Descent and Ascent describe this process, movements from the unity of God to phenomenal multiplicity and the reverse, from multiplicity to unity. These movements are simultaneous, not sequential — two aspects of one divine essence. The supreme moment in Sufism is the sudden shift in perception when a state (in its multiple senses) of exile, of accelerating multiplicity and distance, is experienced as yearning, a re-unifying movement, yearning, towards home, God. The shift is in perception, that is, in the mind. Everything, every object in existence, particularly physical love, move towards this moment. That is the radical subjectivity -love as objective subjectivity - at the heart of Sufism. ("The Idea of a Book"[27])*

*Stairs Room*

*He injured his leg long ago by sky-blue scooter.*
*Since then it is lying in the dust with all other rejected*
*boxes under the electric meter-box.*
*He pats it every day before taking the stairs.*
*You begin ascending from here. It's a staircase math.*
*Just think of marry-go-round and act against gravity.*
*You may turnabout suddenly. If you turn, you begin to*
*descend; that's also math,*
*Why you want to descend?*
*If you ascend, you may get doorbell on the left wall of*
*the floor. Ding-dong; door will open.*
*Take a round and ascend on tiptoe.*
*Now door is closed; open it yourself.*
*Courtyard, sky, pleasant wind, Ursa Major.*
*If you come down, doorstep at the last end,*
*letterbox on right and corner of the old letter.*
*Then the road to go; no end; just walking.*

*I request you – please come*
*And touch to see smooth wooden railing.*
*Just touch lightly dining table, bed and sofa for once.*
*Then straight to courtyard.*
*A vast sky, shooting star. Please sit down just under*
*Rohini. Think that you are merry-go-round;*
*you are dark lighthouse;*

*you are oscillation..... light....sleep*[28] *.*

## *Ascension*

*you'll ascend the stairs slowly*
*on your skirts a golden pile of leaves*
*always you'll be looking at the East crying*

*Always looking at the East crying to be revived*

*waters are yellowing ... your face paling in shadows*
*bending roses bleed bleeding to the ground*
*wait flame like on branches nightingale*
*has water burnt why is the marble bronze*

*From yellow to bronze to crimson to night is the fiery movement of the soul in its ascent.*

*Fire is reflected light in the evening twilight, soon to be replaced by the reflected light of the moon.*

*The nightingale and the branch on which it stands be come one, waiting together.*

*wait flame like on branches nightingale*

*look at the crimson sky turning evening.*
*(Ahmet Hasim* [29]*)*

A trillion plus one
is smaller than a trillion plus two.
in the infinite between two
eyes.

At every step half of what is left. Blue,

plus blue
isn't
two blues, but
but one blue sky
its indifferent eyes
looking in all directions

whereas whereas
infinity exists before a thing happens.

then a thing—
there, a word here,

word, an obdurate orphan.

oh, orphans, orphans
the world is full of orphans,
dispersed longings,

things things things,
as the Prince of Denmark (my fellow orphan)
reads from his book.

"what are you reading, my lord?"

oh, stupid orphan,
why, why do you listen to words that do not happen,

or trying to undo

what's already happened,

trying to join the silence
of infinite zeros.

Oh, my hero,
and and... your cruel kindness.

Spinning backwards (which
in the indifferent eye of the sky is everywhere)
towards the garden. (Camels & Weasels [30])

Murat Nemet-Nejat

~

---

1. In my translation Orhan Veli's poem appears in my poem The Spiritual Life of Replicants.
2.The poem in question is "Untitled – Two," also written in 2017 and translated by Umapad Kar.
3. This poem by the Turkish poet Cemal Süreya appears in my translation both in Eda: An Anthology of Contemporary Turkish Poetry and in my poem The Spiritual Life of Replicants.
4. The translation is by Umapada himself.
5. The translation is by Debatrita Bose.
6. The translation is by Alok Biswas.
7. The translation is by U. K.
8. The translation is by U. K.
9. The translation is by Aryanil Mukherjee.
10. The translation is by A. B.
11. The translation is by R.B.
12. The translation is by A. M.

13. Prow Filling Me (21/3/2012), translated by U. K.

14. Translated by U. K.

15. Translated by R. B.

16. Translated by Bhaswati Goswami.

17. Translated by R. B.

18. Translated by Debatrita Bose.

19. Orhan Veli. I. Orhan Veli, translated from Turkish by Murat Nemet-Nejat, 1989.

20. I. Orhan Veli.

21. The actual text that I read months later was, "All the possibilities are real. Everything that has happened is unreal."

22. Translated by U. K.

23. Translated by R. B.

24. I believe Aryanil also interviewed or wrote about a number of other American poets and artists, including Charles Bernstein and David Chirot.

25. I owe the term 'quantum coherence' to my dear poet and nuclear physicist friend Runa Bandypodadhyay.

26. Mayflies, primitive aquatic creatures, wondrous and comical in shape, grazing, caressing the darkness of water.

27. "The idea of a Book" is the introduction to Eda: An Anthology.

28. Translated by R. B.

29. This poem appears both in the Eda Anthology and The Spiritual Life of Replicants.

30. Camels & Weasels is the poem-in-progress to follow Io's Song.

## Contents

# Dance of Seasonality

## After Drinking the Beverage

Alack path! You are running away instead of me
by crossing both the sides
towards some beautiful eyes of the bust statute
at the junction of tri-roads
When uncertainly the physical leg ran— now in rest
The hopes and joy of the pocket exhausted
in the path along with the pocket.
Only remain the tired legs, like some left out lazy
ice-piece
after drinking the beverage too
Cabin man, Cabin man! Open the gate
The train left the station long back

Then, is that path-preventing- necklace with a red
locket marked 'STOP'
will hang in the neck of the road motionlessly
throughout a long period?
Will it pass away the lonely hours weird fast?
Is it so that my silent legs will mix in engrossed sleep,
without any burden and responsibility!
Hence in the sculptor's infallible hand, horse,
cow-buffalo, steering-wheel,
and my leg would become the image of undistorted
truth
Only instead of wayfarer, the path will run away
towards skyline
Cabin man! Cabin man! Open the gate
The train left the station long ago

## Few Minutes in a Preserved Forest

So many things cannot be grasped by the eyes
Many can be captured
Above all I retain the fickle but secure river in my eyes
The sky lies on the shores of the river
And the hot sand takes bath in the borderline
thrumming water
The glossy red from the leap of the clouds stain
The face of the river in the evening
Then the owls laugh in the bank of the field
Sheaf of paddy swings to pay the salutations
So many things of them cannot be grasped by the eyes
Many can be captured
Above all I retain the fickle but secure river in my eyes

So many things cannot be grasped in the eyes
Many can be captured
Above all I retain the fickle but secure river in my eyes
The preserved forest wreathes the body of the river
The migratory birds return from the
Rainless head of the glue— doesn't make a nest
Illusive deer washes the face in the soothing, silent
water
Butterfly flies close upon the horn
Kingfisher's lip raises waves in the water
Deer runs towards the inmost splitting route of the
forest
Like woman tiara — in the dense and deep
So many things of them cannot be perceived by the
eyes
Many can be captured
Above all I retain the fickle but secure river in my eyes

## Dance of Seasonality

Whoever comes to sing, they all have recited
The reciters danced the season-phase in a band
who has given words to dance they passed their
own dialogue like a disobedient commander
and who is the central-gem-commentator of the stage
he gazed at the microphone with trembling lip and
unwinking eyes
It seems as he forgot to talk for a long period
but the dumb character shouted frequently
in the middle stage by raising the hands

The light-man made himself a prompter aside
And became 'fridge' by continuous stammering
It can be an example of peaceful sudden changes
If the promoter blow out the light in time
He actually hided the grace-dresser's brush
The obligatory grace-dresser came on the stage
"Dear friends! I won't deliver lengthy speech as
chairman
Only one's own circumference...."

Extra-passionate evil designed audiences
Who thought if it deviates from usual routine, they
will build on the stage
a mountain of *Choto-Nagpur*[1] with brick, burnt wood
chunks and old soda bottle
They felt enough elated with praise claps and shining
white teeth
They throw innumerable flowers and colorful
dresses—

## In the dream

You all went to sleep in your own beds at yesterday
night.
I sat down in the bed in waiting with dirty sheets,
oiled pillow and phial of medicine
When it would knock
Someone will open the door with glittering smile
and will address- 'come come'
When the rhythm of feet may arise
When need to welcome by opening the door
and bending the head –'come come'

Almost the night gets over
No one knocks
No more sounds of feet
No one comes— no one comes

Does anyone come?
Anyone stands in the door?
Does anyone sleep in the dream next to the door?
Who comes, doesn't knock
Who comes, doesn't make the sound with feet
Who comes, stand by the door— I am inside in the
waiting

## Jamini and Keya

Jamini da used to hold me by raising both hands
Wherever we met
The earth used to see from a little above
And kept on asking— 'how are you, Taru'?
Keya di visited our house often
Kept rubbing my silky hair gently
Her body fragrance used to spread over in my eyes
And was eager to ask –'how are you,Tara'?
How fast the day and night day by day flies away like
a bee
Jamini da became darker in the noon of night
gradually
Keya di as white as the screw-pine
They don't think now much about Tara and Taru like
previous
I sit down alone to think
while the drum of *Gazan*[2] in *Chaitra*[3] -noon from a far
And the call of the *Kubo*[4] bird start to tune together
'How is jaminida'sTaru'? – 'Keys di's Tara'?

## Human Fossil

Its afternoon now
Around the pity sky and louder winds
Only glistening sunshine
Gravels scattered on the path
And the stature of dark emptiness

There is an infinite field of the wasted crops in the
left end side
The skeleton of the village in the far-away
Someone is walking disorderly through the field
pathway
Doesn't know that everybody left the village
Moved to cremation
There is a dock once turn a little right.
The hot Sand dunes spreading through one mile
The bypass forded river flows in the middle
The fossil of a human is resting in the *ghat*[5] with open
hands
A quarter-rupee for a single ferry
Oh absconder! Will you go to the ferry *ghat*?
Will you move with an image of graveyard fixed in the
heart?
Will you keep the hard stone in the pulp?
That microdot ferry *ghat* gradually turned to radiant
The man is coming out from the human fossil

*All Translated by Nilima Deb.*

# Few Light-years Away

## Why So Late

The drawing-room laid down strait
    on the floor of the large Bedroom.
Folding its knees the Bedroom sits on the sofa
The neat Prayer-room comes
    to clean dusts at Dining-space.
And the fresh bed-sheet of Divan
    is floating in the ceiling as clouds.
Taking shower at early mid-day the bathroom
    went to the common roof.
The store cum parent's bedroom with hope of
    abundant air
    as it opens the south facing window
showers of water from the roof floods the room

To attend door bell in the evening, wiping its palm
    the kitchen opens the door.
The slipper enters the room with whistling
At that moment the perch starts oscillating
    and the antique parrot utters
    "Why so late?"

*Translated by Umapada Kar.*

## Other Sunlight, Other Song

Other sunlight makes the old garden warm.
Other flower in the old tree.
Other honeybee moves in other direction.
Other wind blows strongly.
Other song charms the morning.
Garden stairs look familiar.
Just this, nothing more, remaining are something else.
Other butterfly.
                    You're supposed to come.
That's also other time that passes by.
Other you didn't come at all.
My pain has been reduced by tree.
Other tree, whatever stories of stones –
that's also other stone.
      We'll conceive our child too in some other womb.
Someday I'll become other man
with the care and confidence of the womb.
Other hair, other nail, some other sweat.
                    Oh mother,
it's not your womb, my fascination of birth
with some other embryo.
There is no hard and fast rule to live because I have
                                                            born.
Other labour room is still accessible easily.
Everyday birth takes place for other I, brother, sister.
Other sunlight makes the garden warm.
Other flower blossoms.
Some other song with broken voice.

*Translated by Runa Bandyopadhyay.*

## The Global Stripes: 1

the small snakes while wriggling in between the
holes of teeth
he opened his mouth wide open.
there found, the forest of *Sundarban*[6] with
its mangroves and teaks, the animals
Royal Bengal, honey haunts all with brackish water
getting engulfed in his mouth.
in turn, drawn out from one side the Second Hooghly
Bridge,
the *Farakka*[7] Barrage and canels in huge numbers.
hardly did he spit when some skyscrapers
smashed off the slums so as to erect
themselves high and with intense respiration,
the downtroddens of *Kalahandi*[8] stuck hanging from
his mouth.
with his mouth open he roared in laughter.
ah! his peers too as armies are indulged
nudged someone else or beat some others, went
about in sexual molestation.
the more his mouth was opening with all
ill-rage, the more the thermal power stations crashed
down heavily in thunderous roar.
Arjuna closed his eyes and gracefully
folding his palms said, oh! Krishna,
plead you now, shut up your words...

*Translated by Alok Biswas.*

## The Global Stripes—3

Mother with open mouth, a row of burning furnaces
inside mouth.
Breaking of the earthen pot scattered the hot pulp
throughout; emitting smoke.
Father with incoherent steps; kids smeared with
nasal mucus
throwing their legs towards the void with their mouth
inside the grainless rice pot.
Mother sneezed; the car bomb with R.D.X jelly
blasted off
and stomachs of the children floated in the air like a
shredded cotton.
Gathered clouds set the evening.
Mother laughed. Lasciviour's semen, stool, urine and
saliva of bastard
flowing through the corner of her mouth.
Jingling anklet shattered on her feet. But she was
never angry before.
She used to adorn her forehead with Narayana's
basils.
But now with a slight loss of peace her mouth
engulfing everything
Including homesteads, gardens, cookware, bedding,
whole domesticity too.
The earth is shaking; sensations flying away with
stormy wind;
lakhs of children entering through her lips like flood.
And all are chanting with folded hands - Oh Mother,
please shut your mouth now.

*Translated by Runa Bandyopadhyay*

## Home

### Doorstep

Please come here, it's just one tenth of a minute away.
The borderline of entrance and exit is adorned with
painting.
You may wait for a minute or so.
If you proceed further you will find a sofa.
You have reached from a far, from some lost zinc
civilization.
If you turn about it may seems that you are returning
from the collapsible gate, as the curtain's horses
move away
from the window towards future a far.

### Dinning Space

An experienced man knows the greatness of
eructation.
To say about a big space, chest-frame is the only one.
If you want to laugh heartily, you have to expand your
heart.
You can't imagine how much can be pressed to stuff
the things
from half Rabindranath made of plaster of Paris
to unbreakable food plate of hybrid dog;
from the small brass medal to tongs, left on dining
table.
Tablemats lie down too by folding the table after
dinner.
Please come, sofa is waiting for you.
Sleeping washroom just beside.

Sit down please; the kite is hanging on the opposite
wall.
Coming is easy, going too.
Only the infinite space afloat as light clouds.

## Bedroom

Who haven't thought of entering inside, yet have been
entered,
are suffering from the sound pollution of the
ceiling fan.
Who have already entered long ago,
they have been attached to the foliate design of the
bedstead.
Whoever turning aside from entering at all,
is it worth for them to argue about the colour of the
night lamp?
Since we came here, only love and sleeping.
Everyone is asleep, from the secret locker of the
Almira to wristwatch.
Sleeping tape deck, mosquito net, windows and
doors.
Scales of sleep are asleep and who can get back him
when once asleep?
Sleep may come or may not.
Only corner of the bed-sheet comes flying on the face.

## Drawing Room

Just few minutes; if you come, you have to sit down;
that's our custom.
Even if you don't sit, water, tea and biscuits come.
And if you sit in cross-legged position, mosquitos,
ants, white lizard come.

Housewife is Victoria Ocampo of Rabindranath.
You are flower vase, carpet, coloured woollen ball
and flower.
When you entered, it was dark of evening.
When you will return in the midday,
light green will be still there under the dark of veil.
You may come or go easily.
But few minutes please.

## Stairs Room

He injured his leg long ago by sky-blue scooter.
Since then it is lying in the dust with all other rejected
boxes
under the electric meter-box.
He pats it every day before taking the stairs.
You begin ascending from here. It's a staircase math.
Just think of marry-go-round and act against gravity.
You may turnabout suddenly. If you turn, you begin
to descend;
that's also math,
Why you want to descend?
If you ascend, you may get doorbell on the left wall of
the floor.
Ding-dong; door will open.
Take a round and ascend on tiptoe.
Now door is closed; open it yourself.
Courtyard, sky, pleasant wind, Ursa Major.
If you come down, doorstep at the last end,
letterbox on right and corner of the old letter.
Then the road to go; no end; just walking.
I request you – please come
And touch to see smooth wooden railing.
Just touch lightly dining table, bed and sofa for once.
Then straight to courtyard.

A vast sky, shooting star. Please sit down just under
*Rohini*[9].
Think that you are merry-go-round; you are dark
lighthouse;
you are oscillation..... light....sleep.

*Translated by Runa Bandyopadhyay.*

## Away From Few Light-years

Let it be light
    Let all the voids be light.
If mass may convert into energy
        why not light?
Masses will turn to long-lived light once.

Let the snail be light in its shell
Let the mighty stars originate in our stretched dark
                                        hair
Cluster of rays born from every pore of our skin.

Many voids are in the huge blank space
    and many others will still remain blank.
Physique means dots
    and from the dots of light
  skull of perception ascends,
  some anger, compassion, and sexuality.

Trees are not different one,
    lights like green cocoanut
Nothing as like as chandelier
    all are lamps or light.
Some light-butterflies fly towards few light-years
From the scarf of the darkness the demon's house
      awakes in the illusive tears only.

*Translated by Umapada Kar.*

# Move on Migration

**Photograph**

1
A tiny gravel
And then... ripples, exploration
And then walking along the steps of the sniffy dog
So many ways are open all around, blockages around
so many junctures
And then... past the dusk
Finding at the corner of dumped darkness,
A poem-cum-suicide note, of an assassin,
Ripples once again, he has opted for
Death from the ripples, Subho
The other of our love

2
Down the tracing paper
It's your East Bengal kitchen fences
Come, let's have a snap
*Kishorganj's*[10] *Gyan Gosai*[11]
This is the heaven, the morning sunshine gone
in the sugarfree tea...
Camphor titled Runa Sen's poetry and the waist
Be a snap, at the sound of the black swan's dive
Before it is dark
Ayesha's other smile,
Sensex having shot up
Once again the dream of a resurrection,
Be it a snap

*Translated by Kaushik Chakrabarty.*

**The Other of Shadow**

The other of shadow stands alone
What the public, yes man, fish chops spice
All in one, passing the rain-coat, getting the helmet
Error free
Dumb – doesn't say anything, only serves on
Deaf – doesn't hear anything, even the curses
Opens the door, shuts it, cleans the sofa
Switches the fan on at full speed
What the public, knows will be raped
Still ... changes the bed-sheets
Clinches the teeth, shadow slowly turns to a stone

*Translated by Kaushik Chakrabarty.*

**Face to Face**

let's assemble all the trivial of life inside this tent
black slate, chalk, primer book, *Bibhuti*[12] Einstein
cards chess, hockey stick, tampered football, heart of
a cricket ball
noodles corn, milk cream, green tea onion crispies,
chilled beer
or a bit art – compass needle, paints and brush, stone
chisel
blanket pillows mosquito net, pots pans spoon,
shovel kettle
a few little magazines, Kafka *Illyas*[13], *Bishad Sindhu*[14],
own manuscripts
all these – and then shall I put in some religion too?
so – a bit worship, mantra, iftar easter, and a bit
prasaad
a few cattle goat rabbit spaniel little bit eunuch
and a man with no relationships
now I'll drop on my cot... will sleep read eat drink
sway away the mosquitoes
will dream of Vesuvius, 20,000 leagues under the sea
will shred the dizzies of dream ... leap and jump ..
popsongs, play rugby
ooze out the anger, masturbate, before the ejaculation
will know the primordial name, has it ever matched
the iambic pentameter?
will untie the ropes, unhook the tent ... float the
manuscripts in rough wind
will try to look like Chaplin with the hockey stick
if it's hard, won't have the noodles, will let off the
friendship of the mosquito net
smash and thrash and bundle into football whatever
has been earned in life
I know, now I'd have to stand before eunuchs, will

pacify them to avoid,
and then that man without any relationship will be
my destiny, or me
his... both of us will meet face to face... both of us will
say...
Get lost... you have ruined my entire life

*Translated by Kaushik Chakrabarty.*

**December**

1
when the phantom flower and the fragrance of our
collective living attract us
right at that moment an image from inside the mirror
seeks for leave and turns into the cover illustration
of your Cat Issue
I haven't yet told you anything about
the sharpness of a blind dog and his smelling ability
even the ballads of an accessible bridge,
haven't told you about the mail box of that house
where cures and body are inscribed
I feel experienced when I think of my dead friends
feel like being alive with a technique in this zinc
structure everland

2
the moment a matrix turns to dust, another curls
below the umbrella
a dog lies like an 'o' and matt rests
darkness in every nook, all the blades distressed
how far should go along the cane of an umbrella
to have the taste of death?
upto the salt sea, or blue berry hills, or
even that too is a matrix, a fist full of adultery, oasis,
a spot on alley lost in between the crematorium and
silence

3
a cup of cricket splashes
and thus ends the *Madaari ka khel* [15]
I can't get charred a bit to charcoal
only the waves hum – hippopotamus
haven't got any data of his ejaculation

who's there standing on the tracing paper map
this dashing life, slug
from the summation to showers

*Translated by Kaushik Chakrabarty.*

**Awakening**

The neighboring house wakes up for a murder
Not a word nor an uttering
Neither a whisper or an eerie smell
The sleeps still switches on to sudden lights
The murder is standing beneath the window, in
bright illumine
Window panes rain down from the dream
possibilities
The kid wakes up in the night out of the intoxication
of mum's milk
A mom out of milky white dreams
And drabbing cricket till mid-night
The dad, just asleep – all wake up in the midst of a
murder
The midnight strolls towards the dawn
The dawn picks up a dog sleep day in String Quartet
F major
A silent and motionless murder doesn't block a thing
Just, beside each murder, a neighboring house wakes up
May be it's till dark, or noon, may be dusk or evening
Or may be a formless shapeless time

*Translated by Kaushik Chakrabarty.*

**Dragonfly**

This horse's egg hatched toottie baby
Dawn drooped in a towel
Chocolates of wrong slogans fly out
Of our commune
The sleepless night of a dragonfly on the blade of a
grass
Drooping in the light of the morning star
Let's talk now about recess
*Khoai*[16] there...
Fullmoon snail walks by
Crosses the scribbled age-old corridor
A dusk crawls in with the tune of making
A coffin out of split wood

*Translated by Kaushik Chakrabarty.*

## Ten Deaths

We see our ten deaths
We see minutely a cup of cricket is overflowing
I feel the taste and gum of sugar
Never tell me the stories full of myth
Never push me forward to the phalanx to search the
certainty
Let me see the cold murderer of dear dream
Let me perceive the *Madari*[17] play in bones and
marrows
and the journey of thin leech on flesh and blood
How funny an average born is
We notice minutely a pot overflows with dried seeds
We feel its plasma and sprout
The death series starts
One, two, three....... up to ten...

*Translated by Umapada Kar.*

## Bridge

How far the pillars of a broken bridge can express its
loneliness
How they identify the root of relations and metallic
similes
Moon light slips down on the greyish mosses of the
old bridge
Can it remind some words of midnight with an whore
Ethnic boat is now only a long fibrous shadow after
restlessness
Two hands row the water only, float is statue
Oh! Friend, don't weep and try to open yourself more
than opened already
You become silent after fastening the boat
with the pillars of the broken bridge
The shadow comes out truly
when the moon takes a bath silently

*Translated by Umapada Kar.*

**Black-Board**

A dream on rolling up a shutter
Please wait, don't look at the rugged blanket now,
Don't try to get inside, there the Endless rubs the
blackboard with a duster
A death, wet, lying... killer anopheles fled away
May be ... cultivating... in his home ground, kept his
obedient fingers on the mouse
May be, casting his vote, giving veto, talking about
river's navigability,
Listen to the dead's motionless breathing before you
enter,
Touch the cold cornea, and pray –
Oh dreamless dawn, inertia of the mosquito net,
fill up
All the empty boxes with tick marks
Let me listen to the echoes in the sound system, let
me touch
The blood juice wet death
Not yet healed, not yet gone to sleep inside the
coffin— dead,
As the dreams burn and fly away from the breathless
cage
Shutters roll down

*Translated by Kaushik chakrabarty.*

# Leg of Broken Piano

## Spectacle

The spectacle is not yours; it's of your melancholies
Your melancholies receive pleasures by utilizing this
Whoever wears it, the sorrows disappear as camphor
Let us think, 'A' wore the spectacle
Now it's not feeling anything awkward newly
There is spring in everything, and whatever pained
in past
Are releasing in the white paper
When 'B' uses this spectacle
It starts Startling after startling on his pore of the skin
All the miseries are being scorched in the warm iron
The farina spreads over the horizon of the
tom-canvas
And when 'C' is thinking about wearing this spectacle
Then the singing-tap set up to shower
The major key-notes from the whispering flow-out
on the bucket
The 'C' becomes song by holding the spectacle in hand
The rail of his melancholy doesn't cast anchor further
In any stations

## Suicide Note

The maximum time it would be mentioned in the
suicide note
"Nobody is responsible for my death."—
It is strong pomegranate sensitiveness
One buffalo apathy
To wrap self with a cotton wrapper in plump untruth
Or else to say—
"Everybody else is responsible for my death
except me"—

Either anyone has written such suicide note ever?
If written even anybody would raise hands to salute?

That single note is his last memorandum
Which he wants to submit to all the tamarisk-man

And the suicide with empty note,
Nothing mentioned, just a cat crossed away
Really wasn't it overwhelmed with pomegranate-pain
Was he not been bothered with any vegetal
happenings around?
What can be more than the
Sharp hyena-neglect and wide-vomit

## Silence

Said about two minutes of silence
The Getaway field, tourist clouds
Get going from a long time
Still has not it been two minutes?
I am standing steadily; the branch of memory is
bending
The ramification have bloomed with yellow coral
fruits
Still I am standing; the meeting room is drifting with
the smell of headless demon
Fair memory, the oblivion stands with shoulder-bag
and the help of scratch
The flooded water is entering in that infinite void
The rudder-oar sail-spar are floating away
The speedy train is entering in a wide open tunnel
The deserted runway is spreading over in the back of
the jingling sound
The thousand flights are landing there
Yet two minutes not over?
Doesn't the second bell ring? The chairman doesn't
announce "silence got over, sit down"?
I turned to a tree by continuous standing, will
become woody
I would become stone, please do let me know once
two minutes get over—

## Obstinate

Take it from this circle to that rhombus
Float it from this soup to that vodka
Pass through the rope-way from this bank across this
flashy stream
Yet the imminence is not amendable to persuasion
The inevitability may note about offering stokes, or
flattering
Its look like striking, deceiving four-six-*anna*[18]
So obstinate never forget
The destiny talks the same again and again and sings
the same song
The obstinate writes the same words in the whole
page with whole ink of a pen.
Pertinacious, let's forget
Will change your blood
Will pluck your eye brow
Will adorn you as a clown in the fair of *Shivagazon*[19]
Let's forget the tenacious
Yet the imminence is not amendable to persuasion
Also not for increasing the starch in the blood too
Not even mix the Mexicana poppy in the body oil.
The obstinate speaks the same word, chews same
song
Concentrates or yawns on particular poem,
The obstinate had sheltered like a tent in me.

## Fear and Ohm's Law

We can be confused with the fear and unknown symbols
of an equation.
How much can mean by an equality of an equal sign in
between two wings of an equation?
Once the scary lightening of the left end side plays its rule, the secrets of right end side increases its resistance by condensing. It is very urgent to break down the mystery glamour. Again once the queries of juvenility peeps, the vainness cross the limit of over-pertness. The renovation may be struck by lightning in huge potential difference. The body wakes up in fright if the mystery leaks. Suddenly the symbol of the middle one raises its length like a rope and turned to the runway. The dry dusty pulp of creepy domestic life lies on the one hand. And the other side allows the deserted ship to chew the spike of the fear in search of suitable resistor. We bend on the Ohm's law— either there is anything wrong!

## The Star and Constellation

### Polaris

Still you are invariable when all are troubled by changing the position gradually. There is no amazement mark in your perseverance .But the earth is rotating. The axis of impetus is moving through the boundless stop. We are tactfully fixed in the limitations instead of moving round and round. May be you have seen steady everyday due to the mannerism of the affectation of instability by revolving repeatedly- in same sky, in same half circle, in same flow-tide or ebb-tide, in the different truth of daily routine.

### Ursa Major

Not only the seven saints, it may be you, me, he or another four persons. May be white horse, pig, lion, ostrich — the seven. Or else may be the timid king of seven century or may seven variety flowers. The joyous fact, they survive in the chapter, 'The stars of sky' of science book. What is the interest behind such surviving in queries? We can memorize the departing of mother. She was promised— will be a star after the death, may be a mole on the body of Ursa Major. One day we can become the seven stars who express our fear about the lights of this city, who raise queries about the purification of drinking water, or raise the flag in the redressing of air pollution. Most probably it may reflects from any of this great bear as some Nishikanta, pitiful, timid is almost dead before dying. He was accustomed to writing poems in fear. That's Siddiqui— very peevish, who loves painting more than teaching. But never could complete a drawing. That, that's the Angela— a beauty, so smiley, used to share love to all either deserves or not. The end is suicide. Exactly such seven man of deep story will enlighten their existence in the counter established Ursa Major.

## Orion

The handsome in wide belt, the knife which hangs from the waistband is restless like the leakage flute of cowherd. Coward— with bow in hand, the arrow with strong poisonous essence dived in once coming closer to the leg of that afternoon girl. Not only the love, looking for something more, gets something, get killed immediately. Orion— time harms, time only saves, all about the puppet show of time. Orion— walks on, sleeps at dawn, dreams, stay awake at night in the field of harvest. Orion— it's sweating in the body, sometimes in gladiator, sometimes knight, again sometime acts as diplomat (home pigeon litter). It's not fault to think it as scarecrow today. Orion— handsome, coward, man like a scarecrow or not a man.

## Scent of Demise

When stand before the death face to face
The strong scent of camphor spreads over from the
ordinary domestic life

Barin da might have realized this state exactly
It can be asked of him what about the height of the
palm tree in the dessert

How depth need to dig the sands for a single sip of
water
He may utter in witticism 'wow! What a color, what
a shine!'
Nobody can even imagine before, a coma has its own
color too
The vibrant smell of camphor in the black trunk is
enough if we want to step behind
A coma colored flag will fly in the air if we want to
look forward
Everybody wants to realize a little about the state of
Barin da at least once
When the moving forward man steps back,
the scent of camphor smells in his body strongly.

*All Translated by Nilima Deb.*

## The Blood-soaked Grains

by the side of the victim there may accumulate some
blood which being dry
may turn copperish or go in blackish.
large flies will buzz around and buckets of
water from police may wash out the fears and scorns
born out of bloodshed.
may there be posted an observatory camp
after the act of assassination smeared with
bloodstains.

nothing can be made clear as well—
how much grievances raised.
who flared up the anger-shell with a flash of
matchstick.
that the level of degrees of serpentine grates cannot
be made clear.
who the fellows that despised them and
to what extent they despised.

a man victimized lies apparently silent after much
awakening,
where the forensic fly-team overpowers the
dried-out blood
with vigilants around.
what an investigation ! the murdered sleeps while
locals sighing a relief,
none is to mourn.
the motif de venge behind the fallen is not yet known.
the mercury scale remains unknown,
the blood-soaked grains are only
getting stoned...

*Translated by Alok Biswas.*

# The Other Spring

(Poetry No. 1, 2, 7, 10, 23, 33, 41, 47, 48, 56)

79-88

## The Other Spring

### Poetry No. 1

A little fly of a bird in the wide sky
The lonely star rose across the pear of eyes
Wait till your normal red dust of twilight
Perceive an evening opening the bra-hooks quickly

Waiting by looking at anywhere as usual
Someone have been waiting in between the waiting
As a naked truth that song was sang with waving the
handkerchief
Now it wipes the neck silently to remove the stinky
sweat smell

None was for wearing bangles
None was for tightening up the skirt at waist
The anklet sprang up all by itself
And stumbled with musical clattering

Now rapid surging up navel at the dance floor
How fast it can rise and fall, how do you expect!
When the evening came down in little bit earlier
Keep the client's sweetheart appeal like an apple

*Translated by Umapada Kar.*

## Poetry No. 2

Whatever comes, comes from inside.
A little glass a stone little bit delight.
Sun-melted shine could be understood from outside.
Continuous jingling waterfall,
slowly drying vaginal musk,
and a light spin reaction of all of them

All enter inwards.
Hot sour salt and ice from outside.
Cleaning the soured time, the comparative words
can still keep them shinny.
No change in the internal volcano,
only it may spread around any moment.

Submarine or greedy periscope is coming and going
from the interior or towards the innermost.

*Translated by Runa Bandyopadhyay.*

## Poetry No. 7

when the ear-rings of colourful snake glitter,
a missed call on pretty hip and in
pompous evening the water swallows a
boat a star and watery foams...a crescent
moon grows out of sand-born semen...

the tent and the peg remain awake, if slept, time will
wear them out.
the wheezing wind's hybrid hype
after its chat, takes a sound sleep
on headstand yoga. the torn tents flap in air...
the young clerks run a groaning tryst
with staggering scooter.

here reaches the chorus band of day's last omnibus.
where rests the dreamy wedding *Sherwani*[20].
do sing now and bit drums, let *Uloopi*[21] dance.
Hurrah!
welcome all kitchen utensils,
a bath with Vodkaine. if the head totters,
a penalty fine of five. oh dear Bengali...

*Translated by Alok Biswas.*

## Poetry No. 10

worn with raincoat the Spring solicits, in
lucid and shortcut tone, 'excuse me'.
sunlights slumbered as Kumbhakarna
on all paths and having shattered walk on walls.
the paths being exhausted, it's epiglottis held out
with a treacherous command to the Spring to stand
by on rest.
some flowers some fragrance or a little chewing nuts
could'nt be offered as present to the Spring.
the whirlwind went round the meadow.
by whim's wrong, hypertension hovers on
latitude and longitude.
the time of B.P. limitlessly on climax and
the annual report floating on in customary habits,
folding the camp-bed at dawning,
bidding farewell in drowsiness came close to
drunken burning-ghat.
when the auspicious birthday will sleep in
wooden coffin,
say 'excuse me', once again, oh Spring!
give me a chance, be it half, dear Spring!

*Translated by Alok Biswas.*

## Poetry No. 23

shuffled is the dawn having tested of bitter gourd,
sorting them out.
will be gathered in rows at Babumarket at 7 a.m.
four divisions, in each full green basket
some ochros...right at 8.23 a.m. warm-rice on which
lying brinjal-fry.
the local train at 8.43, but drowsiness still
continues due to the effect of strong Alzolam...
roll call at 10.17, with primer count-downs
the moons with adhesive are stuck in all
departments...then comes tiffin along with tomato
sauce, sweet Halva
along with trump card games surrounded with
colleagues' outcries...
at second round cropped up birds' wings.
someone else turns to be a flying wing or a dash or
stick or hazard...
again shuffled in pale-sunny response
numerous ravels picking up fullglass drinks...
people do open with a slow pace
the *Tekka*[22] card that beats nice, thrown off
*Saheb*[23] card splendidly acts, finally
*Bibi*[24] card excellently defeats all others...
the tottering shirts, though feel sleepy with
heavy victorious pockets, the shoes too
will advance with shuffled playing cards
in the full-fledged evening...

*Translated by Alok Biswas.*

## Poetry No. 33

Window doesn't know what I want to write sitting by
window.
The crow sitting by window is not sure about
whether I write myself only or not.
The areca tree wants to understand
what I can or want to write.
Their companion is crucial before being drifted away
by spring.

The tree could hear, the crow could hear, grills and
windows too.
Let milepost's ear hear from them
what I have written so far.
Oh, silent spring you can wake up now
through wind, to awaken too.

No greater parameter is there to know
whether I write myself or not.

*Translated by Runa Bandyopadhyay.*

## Poetry No. 41

the loaded pitcher taking a hint of evening as
darkling turns itself down.
the same how nicely and incessantly
pours forth light. the sudden change
of background yields the opportune's
flowery crackers. now the bats 'n titmouse
retreat again on their seemingly
*Ardhakurmasana*[25] woodnest.
even if the curtain is removed, the blind sun
not brought out. it was about to see, but
could not, so much sunbeams.
who removed the curtain, who swept away
the individuality of correlation.
a basket of interlinks enters the room when the
duplicate key opens it.
the shirts get dried in part-time sunlight.
in curved sunbeams the fresh smile
made clear by the artist's brush on one
side of the face.

*Translated by Alok Biswas.*

## Poetry no. 47

Sleeping stairs make Nilu, sleeping in every step, Nilu in every step.
A bead is rolling down through his every So-La-Si.
Sound becomes delighted on every step by thousands of rolling beads.
As the rolling speed increased, water jingle filled the ears.

There're only images and sounds, let us talk about thoughts now.
It's not right to say that awakened steps will think nothing.
It's thinking whether dreams were there behind light sleep.
Beads' run more than their thoughts to win the race.

Three streams are flowing through steps,
of water, of milk and of blood, overlapping nowhere.

*Translated by Runa Bandyopadhyay.*

## Poetry no. 48

the speech sleeps under head as pillow.
the head remains awake nighttime over.
three words against war not be expressed to a suitble
utterance.
the head is reeling round the world thinking on 'n on.
is dream possible in wakefulness?
he may laugh the last laugh dreaming of Alzolam,
and at the end of it may pour
water down on funeral-ash after removing
all anxieties from the warmth of pillows.
salute after salute to the wakeful night.

the poem appears in awful sky and disappears too
with suddenness.
the head still lying awake enlivens the body,
a light ringlet-sleep in dawn
and in some words born out of the pillow's cotton,
appears *Falguna*[26],
whereby found one after another the flower *Palasha*[27]
bearing the news of war.
the media madness dance at the search of fitting
words.
the sound-sleep breaks up suddenly on warm pillows.

*Translated by Alok Biswas.*

## Poetry no. 56

a whistle's heart opens out, to what decibel can reach
its scream.
a stubborn train which was to go to the West, how far
can it run to the north.
the driver is but sweated with much labour,
his son too who lives Bangaluru doing IIT job hardly
sleeps at night.

a beer bottle from decent freeze, the glass brimming
full.
the doctor never accepts this as the sanitary basin is
littered with
black-stool and the professor after seeing
the gateways to several hells, involves
forbearance in some translations of Galib's poems as
he got obsessed in love of him.

the horses on curtains not remain screened, rather
run adrift to inferno.
the childhood days too run out of ink
due to over-simplicity. how much he deemed the
Platonic philosophies of his
grandfather as well as grandmother.
his knees stuck deep under frowning
moustache of his private tutor.

if mother calls, who to respond is not known to
gleaming Spring.
if father, not shown such cadence even in SMS.
two sweety endearing hearts can barely sit before
internet chatting
and the topic goes on till the time limit fixed on the
beak of waiting Hornbill.

Translated by Alok Biswas.

# Vowels to Bow Words

## Hyphen

I knelt down before a hyphen
With finger on my chin, I sat there for hours
My desire thickened into film
The film moistened and triggered droplets trickling
down
on a full-stop
An exclamation mark leapt up from there
A car dashed out taking sharp triangular bend
and enquired about the access and way out from the
proscenium
Thereafter, it froze into a question mark before the
collective eye
A pair of trains will be on display before raising the
curtain
Overlapping squeal will fade away fast
A thunderous applause will burst on the theatre
that never had a rostrum
I was sitting once
I am sitting now, as I might sit on in future
Holding a hyphen's hand...

*Translated by Bhaswati Goswami.*

## Thermometer

The Guillotine cuts the light
The darkness pushes its neck into it
Created a piece of wasteland by rubbing eraser on
deep darkness
Wants to make a room with ridge

Our future light is bright
Sun bathing two-four *kharisa*[28] are on the ridge
Our darkest possibilities are the Pyramids
The metallic moon decays on the ridge

However I extend my hand, It still beyond my reach
However I retract my hand, can't get the relief of pain

I do have a fever, thermometer doesn't know

*Translated by Umapada Kar.*

## M

Finally imagination self-referred
Blowing away black soot from the dwindling wok
Sits humming in front of a clean oven
Throw-in-some-grain faith cooks to soft floral rice

Why one brings up rice always before being spoiled
Rice never gets it, muggy and sweating streams
Sourfaced, carbon copied land of rickets
Your near ones your loving plotting folks

Imperative to become a half woman, pregnant at
least once
Returning pale dream-pukes of the early months
Blue sky beaded with moonshine's mercurial
pendants
Light descends to lit up vaginal floodgates

Hrrr hurrah landfall baby yay yay jubilatory
Man's ma all the mummering immersed maidenfolk

*Translated by Aryanil Mukherjee.*

## Wooden Birds Earthy Suspicions

Wooden birds and earthy suspicions never rest on
a perch

Spring heralds even if cuckoo coos in the wrong
season
Let denials whatever be, cloaked in that
mischievous smile

A ribbon has been tied around the cat's neck,
replacing bell
A moderate pair of scissors is all set for the
ribbon-cutting
Panicky rats run helter-skelter

A line drawn along another can be straight or inclined
Some lines make a sharp mother's face
The two dots lingering between the voids are but half
a chance
From yet-to-be-over graph of life
Rough and tough

The hazy lines can lead to a triangle
Or perhaps a rhombus
Then all the crests will be illuminated with
unfathomable light

The wooden birds and earthy suspicions will
mutate into rocks ...

*Translated by Bhaswati Goswami.*

## Print Out

The lavishness of an earthen orange could not be
gauged from it's extract
Mouth-watering or salivated mouth, brimming with
juice and dyed in a superficial shade
Familiar errors in glow, matured by unknown
hormones and identical in appearance
Stony charm of the skin does not care for the deep
emotions of the pod

The myth of an orange-hearted delicate pod wins
over all
Let icicles of cumin-coriander be dipped in orange
tint
If humid, might as well travel down the archetypal
*Rhotang*[29] pass
Icicles become pollens of love in erotica, shattering
frame

Everything that could not be avenged, calls for
resemblance
Sourness demands more acidic cells
Concentrate wants sweet stings
A few of the leaves squeeze out virgin nature while
hooked to the stalk
And, orange suffers from orange-fever as Sankara's
mom fondles with a leaf

A wry smile in the mirror fails to register acidity or
insipidness
Authorized by the cuckoo chick lives on as the
nestling of an unknown bird

*Translated by Bhaswati Goswami.*

## Around the Flower's Neck

The fleeting time initiated from Big Bang to the
present
Minus,
The moving caravan-like -time, from my birth to this
nanosecond
Is the left out time difference
That holds the fantasy of a painted pomegranate bud

A delighted dinosaur sprang up, to open a door
A mongoose with a snake in trail waited there
A part of time drifts to the desolate ground
Where no entertainment as 'time' had ever existed

One can walk up to the portico
Wear a comical grin stretching ear to ear
The crickety thoughts of inappropriate time lies in
the care of eternal time
And the chime of a fruit tightens noose around the
flower's neck

*Translated by Bhaswati Goswami.*

## The Cuckoo Sings

Green apple dipped in erotic tongue lush and juicy
Tinkling s.m.s. drifts over seven seas
And, passionate words dyed in the hue of forbidden
fruit
Makes a titillating cover

Whatever lives in forest, lives in mind too
Trees and shrubs, long-dead-woodcutter, wood and
chop
Images or lack of it
The petrified thoughts of a philosopher becomes an
ornate wristlet

Entwined thread runs into the loop of relationship
and oozes resin
Mines have been laid by the rebels, warriors, victors
and vanquished
Smoke billowed out, faces, torso and rest of the relics
were charred

There, dance-moves swirl in the rhythm of
cum-rum-pum-pum
Radha never dances
Ever-changing foot-steps get ferried gradually
Jingling ankle-bells sink slowly in the moron called
brain

La la laila milkmaid, milk-butter-ghee
Existence in fat, living in marrow, travel in blood and
trek-trekking in sweat
Cum Come September, the cooing of cuckoo
overflows forest, mind and elsewhere

*Translated by Bhaswati Goswami.*

## Spark

Birds are kissing their offstings
        with some tips
How will they practise the music at dawn!
When will they just flyaway
after the completion in search of fruits and stories of
                                                insects
In what range of twilight they will come back
How will they sleep in the lap of the tree boughs at
                                                night!

Morning wakes up from sleep by the cooing of
                                cuckoos in Spring
Listening to the cuckoo's sweet and delicate song
                                        with relish
            the forest become gratified
You were somehow engrossed in something else,
and didn't stretch your hand though I desire you to
                                                touch
Didn't expose any interiors of the depth

Color and resonance of morning
may now be washed out by another spark...

*Translated by Umapada Kar.*

## While Going off or Coming down

You are counted twice
While coming and
going out

Rose-water was sprayed
An otto-pot was held in your hand
and a color-coated smile on face

No visiting hours notice board
was clicked on the wall
visits forever

Clouds like the tenth symbol of playing cards wait
upon
with margosa-scented air and water purified to
rinse and wash
with urgency for falling in drops

They touch the ground immediately before the storm
as they are to fall down
Don't skid off while going out or coming

*Translated by Umapada Kar.*

## In The Shadow of a Milkyway

A shaft of sunshine has illuminated the Milkyway
The shadow has paused in it's path
A neighbourhood went to slumber
The milkiness prevailed still

Fan and breeze
Were seated together at a banquet,
Gobbling up bell-chime to the brim,
They ended up in a meek lament

Stairway is the new address of warmth
An Iguana climbs up and descends in late spring
Only to be modified into a round docile doormat in
winter

Speckles of nose-rings in array,
Lying somewhere between blue and green
Before getting friendly to each other
The celebration for ring appears unexpected
And gets washed by a peg or two

Sandwiched between Chayan and Chayanika
The aged father walks on a stick
Throwing stress all around—
And stands in the shadow of a Milkyway...

*Translated by Bhaswati Goswami.*

## Song of Fall

Who, that he yearns for other's good
Who, that he renounces luxury for others
As one joins in a chorus,
What would be the music that harmonizes most?
A victim in this maze of questions,
The aimless cloud absconds

Dos everyone celebrate *Poush-Pitha*[30], when flowers bloom?
As the barn bursts with a rich reap of paddy
Does every household partake of the ritual rice of autumn harvest?
The oblique sky encircles in affection
As the kite loves flying
The pebbles descend down the hills and physique

Who, that he vanishes stealing someone else's smile
Who is the 'Quasimodo', that mourns for the tears of other's
in an unknown address?
What does he do there, hold or leave behind—
The questions are meaningless
And the hope for answer is bleak as an empty pitcher

The monsoon has deluged
The coronet of spring has left a transient glance
The song of fall is in wait,
after sowing seeds of love...

*Translated by Bhaswati Goswami.*

# Floating Twilight of River

## Walnut

Eyes are walnut

The drawn eyebrows are curved like
the bow like bent-train of morning

I have to go to the light and darkness of the shadowy
bushes
Though we declined to go

Break down the brickbats
The tear drops

Rage and affection
Go hand in hand, and dangling a teardrop

Time could not decide whether
It would fall or not

Raising laughter face

Still it says 'good morning'

Eyes just go out for walking

*Translated by Manik Saha.*

## If Comeliness is Added

In changed sunlight
The morning which is the chirping of *Ishti Kutum*[31]
Yellow of the *kutum*[32] is a little changed too
Eyes sustain
Our sustained eyes are like parallel lagoons
That want to change themselves too

Nail, hair, feathers of head grow every day
And decrease in same proportion the creeping
comeliness
Moist of *Jamrul*[33] as well
As an alternative to bath
'Saona bath' wants to lie in Lazy cloud Tub

Let's judge the color of evening *Dopatta*[34] according
to its intellect
Girdle of *Cheli*[35] goes to the desi bar abrading the
ground
Whether it is the sun or the moon or a star
Let it be selected in Mass voting process
Where fat is enough outside but intellect is meager

If Grace is added to the changed cornea,
Intellect will become camphor.

*Translated by Manik Saha.*

## Cosmic Bell

Bell and silence oscillating alongside
Ding-dong and its resonance...and the next..
My ears advancing with small steps
into its labyrinth.

Language confessing its limitation to sound,
And spreading its wings to fly in rows.
My listening to sound is tuned in the same direction
of advancing shoreless sea.

When static cosmic bell,
nature of silence,
and my silent desolation
become sea-waves on one another
I want to be deaf.
I want to fuse my remaining feathers
with the wet hair of Niagara as a part of the nature.

*Translated by Runa Bandyopadhyay.*

## Prow Filling Me

The moon goes below poverty line in the depths of the night. Shredding a few buffalo-clouds it swells in country liquor. In the darkness of zero kerosine, a snatch of butter moonlight makes the woodman sex up. Ricket yawns, bats suck on a shriveled left-aubergine...

The stammering myna is lame, flood-ravaged teen, her part pride; one leg jutting out from below her frock, I said, let me spread some holy water. She doesn't retort, transforms to a hill. Huts turn mansions ... moon drunk on country wine, it descends into the dark waves...

The whistle brings out the kids. Bare little ones, they drill ... drill kids naked breast await... funny flowers patch the junkyard...

08/09/2011

Mirrored face distorts to its limit. Stay-put there. In the meanwhile evening...

In dawning amber a couple of morning-walkers talk about life. Gradually evening...

In terrace garden pots creper-oleanders cajole and their chameleon moves bring evening...

These evenings swaying with oleanders, shading minasops, flickering flowers light up love...

I told ma long back I'm coming... have to tell wife now... my sons (24/ 09/ 2011)

Who to put beside whom, flute next to snake, or the other way. A hood fine with color charms. The conch blew, and touchy time stands erect on its tail... hiding copulating memory, where I want to go often... but can't quite

The genie comes during sleep time, and the genie leaves... to and fro magic of the fluent breeze... a thousand pigeon wings clap... ruptures sleep, sulking amongst the bamboo clumps

Can't cheap describe sweet me myself. The bags to show open line up... every cauldron filled with bee buzz ... nostalgic morns with two myna's salute peck... when some day it's three the third one's a genie

Radha and flute are inseparable... I can be a sleeping snake beside them... the flute knows perhaps a bit of my memories hold on to shivers

22/10/2011

As the outcast in me implodes, consciousness dances too. At a distance stands Nabadwip and the river.

Should have been a neighborhood browbeat, turned out stray poet, saw Baudelaire taking of his hat to bow. 'Waste land' watches from the nook.

I walk on the left or right, no I never walk almost, afternoon herons and evening-bats carry its parameters. A little further from there the crows from dawn shred my poetry manuscript.

Haridas knows how long I have been a trier on the banks of poetry. He knows his clever pen hasn't been to prostitutes. Dumb bystander outside the red light streets.

When dogs bark, the fox scrambles in me. I have tried to feel the pulse of poetry, feel love's lard and lust. Haridas stands out there crying at times, sometimes a laughing jester, at other times unrolling the kite-spool to remake poems or in the midst of a freeze...

25/ 10/ 2011

*All Translated by Aryanil Mukherjee.*

Few words may be exchanged with the combustible substance at the time of cremation. Keeping it at distance... Ash-colored stories come out from the rudeness of death... My face turns to red due to generation of burns... From the core of heart comes out a little 'Ah' and cold groaning sound... This is visible... But matters nothing... Buddha was then at *nirvana* with a smile in his face and closed eyes...

My friends will go someday for your cremation. That also I... the Palas-peer, the Shimul-peer... A self song of crematorium will be played on... due to the nostalgia of my meeting with the combustible substance a long ago... that also a music... assembling together, blending smoothly...

Now, words are for the light. The particles of light sprayed from the crematorium may recognize me at a glance... I am at the center of light with burning sensation... let's go now to any direction...

21/3/2012

The alloy of ornament mixes up with words. As the day and the dawn involve the night and evening respectively with few chats. In course of conversation the mamma becomes deepening, calmness too. The mood soaked with tears out of nickel-plated weeping is a lyric...

Salutation offered for oneself, even bowing down. They are bread as like as them. Rolling, baking and then puffed up with warm air... as if it is compulsion ... the smell of sweat of the bread... bread croton... the eyes, noticing from the hillock, are made of stone. If tears come out, still it is not felt...

The confined words acidify me or settle as stone being fermented. In thinking process it is a Crow, otherwise a Drongo... song of Atulprasad... The gravid Cow tries to recollect the poetry of the stoical bull about the setting Sun... perhaps it can't...

12/04/2012

*Translated by Umapada Kar.*

## Not Eye But Three Playing Cards for Three

Poetry no. 5

Where desire to be a stone is the joy of heart.
Where desire to be an elder is not by ageing only.
Where only liver pain rings but not the veena.
The tan naevus sparkles like a diamond when light
falls on it.
Wasn't there a naevus birthmark
on the back of your waist?

Light of firework is no more.
Sandal doesn't fit to the foot.
Time moves on beyond slipper or sneaker.
Graceful feet with clip-clap sound.
Fly in stony way
without any sound.

## Poetry no.17

When 3:2 equals to two.
When guerrilla-wind:eclipse equals to cricket Greg
brothers.
When dollar versus domination is nothing but a
greasy bamboo.
Arithmetic enumeration starting from mathematical
table of three rains alike.
Sensex also hits the same height.

If *Aila* hits hard, why Sita has to restrict herself
to be ashamed of her hip, calf and ankle
in their role of sixteenth.
Seven looks foolish after three.
It seems that seven seas want to be relieved from the
glory of myth.
Seven worlds.
Seven stories.

Here cultivation with rainwater; grammar doesn't
retreat from war.
Here grape: vine to sing to dance to spread...
Here only versus and versus and versus...
Which could be named after *Alvida*.[36]

Poetry no. 23

When the darkness arrives by cloud's reaction.
When your departure brings the darkness.
When cloud's arrival become synonymous with your departure.

Supporting on air leaves and branches are shaking.
A tumultuous quivering in stems and main root too.
But I couldn't perceive it.

I need to light a match
to see the hesitation of the darkness
to see where elephants of *Dalma*[37] could be missing.
Where they can lower their trunks like aerial roots.

What a joke, when toothbrush stands in front of the false teeth.
Lethargy fills the smoker's lungs carefully.
Still going means going but both coming and darkness
are to make cloud's reaction on playing.
Roots get wet once again.

*All Translated by Runa Bandyopadhyay.*

# Light of Scythe

## Sailor

I hide my room.
And cut the windows to keep the pieces in my hidden
pocket.
The single door is wide open
that I keep in my breast pocket.
I keep the walls, floor and ceiling in a bag.
The room is no more intact.
No one else can enter this room.
Some people may say
'A room was here!'
I'll remind them 'yes, there was'.
I'll show them the existence of the fragmented room
if required,
from the pocket from the bag from the heart.
They will jump too.
But they can't enter the room, can't decorate it.
I'll become a sailor by sailing the room.

**Cheroot– 4**

I'm a white page in her pleasing gaze.
I mix sugar with black letters
and filter it.
The cup brims over
with a no signal gesture.
Stimulates poem to gladden the heart...

I'm lovelorn in her morning mind.
Wintryphysique blossoms the 9 o'clock.
I throw my gloves to float in Jasmine sunshine.
Leaning on the youth of white page.
Thinking whether de-ornamented Sita is the poem!

As soon as I touch her cold modesty,
creepy door
opens at once...

## Ginger Chips - 1

I'm the floating lamp in the sky, you're the Picasso's
Guernica.
You live a modest life ...

My palm tree is as much picturesque
as your eucalyptus
tall and sad.

Your swim and my first foreplay, unknown to swim.
Sweet and sour on every reed.
Hot like ginger chips.

You're rhythm of the censer-dance.
My steps don't match with *bhangra*[38] dance.
I can't hide my desires.
You're screen of frothy laugh in slippery excursion.

Time gallops before afternoon.
Like a buffalo afternoon sets off too.
With a foolish laugh, time makes us nude.
With a useless duel between me and you.

## Crazy

So long I didn't write you about the long shadow of twilight.
So long neighbours didn't say about the unparalleled evening walk.
The sleeping Monster day by day burned away in the woody city.
The kite-spool opened countless knots to release long thread
without a kite...

Old fairy tales sat beside the rice-bin.
Air returns to tryst from the corner with its flying hair.
Hands will squeeze out the sky now to bring stars in poor's plate.
A calm mother will look for her children...

The lost language looks for its lost slipper in the luggage.
Whether it will find or not can't be understood even after enough
flight.
*Ghat*[39] returns bow-filled domesticity of the sailboat.
Where will it go, where is the goldmine....

So long I didn't read you, born with an ordinary spoon in mouth.
So long I didn't pat the grains not even once.
Who has placed pitcher-full of delight in the brocade of crazy eyes.
Hey Midnight, unbutton the dress even the inner one right now...

## Kimia – 3

Charisma of dream is only in renewal.
A single song covered with crotch, a single line
covered with eyeliner.
Chase insane, chase bulls, snakes, elephants,
chase daggers.
And my inability to chase away.

As much sexuality of Khajuraho's broken nose.
As dream opens venetian blind to conceive.
Opens the darkness under the stairs.
Frock to 'sharee', ornamented elaborately.
Feeling thirsty, calling... calling continuously.

Wings of bird spread dream-seed to become our *Rai*[40].
Hump in throat, mucus in eyes, grass on nose and
ears with no membrane.
Leased breast just like human.
Waterfalls start to hawk the dreams before being
mesmerized.
And I float out of gravity
to feel the God particle...

## The Amulet Pen -2

When wits are lost, birds forget to call.
Peacock's plumage can't even see itself in thick mist.
Before being lost the awaken city can't help
but falls asleep in slowly collapsing voice...

A call to mom opens up details somewhere,
Opens up unread waterfall
rather than detailed description.

Eye gaze hints not to say anything.
Water within water set me adrift with sudden flood.

Boundless nature assures us to give the whole thing
to someone.
Drunken *Mahua*[41] -movement of accumulated colour
on the canvas.
May be there, may be not, no dawn on the clock.
From the thought that birds will call soon,
A glowing point in lethargy of thick mist
reminds me the picture of the lost and found
column...

## The Amulet Pen-4

Reindeer comes out of the match.
Blue sheep from the moneybag.
*Kirtan*[42] -procession in the kite-flying courtyard
rollicking by illusive and unbearable *ref.*

From Shiva phallus to *Nagkeshar*[43] to spoil the Shiva
festival.
Such a freshness to ignore even the *Nataraj*[44] too.
Gathering *Yajna's* firewood one by one to fuel my
interior.
And returning horses from the peak of the globe to
neigh.

Soothing comfort may tear out in *matrabritta*[45]
meter.
The ejected arrow is missing since it went for
hunting.
Deer call eagerly to be pierced.
Horse demands for rebirth before the *Yajna*[46] .

The blue sheep has painted the moon inside canopy
gaps today.
Son and reindeer have come to sit on the lap of
moonlight...

## Primordial Walking – 5

Vacillation in its own language of evening lamp
translating the evening to tell
the desire of domesticity beyond its image.

The chord creates the bowstring's tension easily.
Large portion of deer's body
in the mouth of long python.
Moon rises with screaming of its slim sky-faced legs.

Salts of wall melt in moonlit bath.
Fall drop by drop on dead leaves.
Chirping of cricket slough off slowly.

Figure of the remaining shadow
deny the myth with a pose of uttering hymns.
Eyeliner of evening lamp writes
the compassion of language....

## Bubbling

When I turn a water page, poems float up.
And lost somewhere with small waves of water.
It continues until my own grows within me.

As the kite-spool opens its thread, poems start flying.
Its tremulous wave in random wind remains unclear.
As long as I shake myself by shouting hurrah.

The flying dove of interior can't be understood from
exterior.
Few drops of rain from cloud make the poetry-bird
to fly by overcoming its inertia.
Set the sail with mastto sail through river.

Negation becomes wet and lustre scatters by
crossing the hazy light.
A ringing tone synchronizes with my dizzy brain.
All my dryness become aqueous lowland.

As long as a bubble bubbles inside....

*All Translated by Runa Bandyopadhyay.*

# Jingling of Sandman

## Jingling of Sandman

1.

With the cocktail of Somalian sunshine and Japanese
moonlight
Introspective is today's Evening glasses on the table
Who gave unasked ice cubes in the glass
Who gave majestic dim blue light
Who are they, mixed the sprinkle and wave in the
served-glass?
Drink to the lease, enjoy the music and dance as you
wish
Rampant beat of song and sound, ho-ho
Dry lips dangling under the raised armed tree
Talk, and kiss, and tumble into joy, and roll down
again—
Guard, trembling thigh, switching on the Pull / Push
button just Stand on

2.

What could be lost? May be a *'Malkosh'*[47] of Marijuana
chillum
At least the flying iron duck from the smiling porch
It's troublesome in the sudden rain, still some
shivering swans with pleasure
Crowing of two crows singing of the sun
melted the gluey sleep-joy of our dear neighbor.
The city rose when the sun gives its ray at 8 o'clock,
the Aunt's House

Hawkers with their trade cry, jolly sales persons
Roasted sliced loaf and nickel knife for jam

The stubborn rider, the naughty hotty Niko-park-love
kadambushi (bow/ bend) to all of you, salute to the
kids
Let's start another day— Let's start left-right-left

3.

No Rome is burnt, no Niro plays the Banjo
All go away, hand in hand, rows of beef and pork
shops in market
and the morphine trees
Different caps, United Nations' number, hair passport
The open navel light slants on the jacked air
Delicious thighs and handful valance, silent story in
pomegranate juice
The police or the jockey is afraid of the rape of the
sister

Horse runs towards the horizon, fluttering at night,
setting out in the morning
Hunt for footsteps, market catchment notice
Hearts should be mixed with all colors, standing in
front with furnished boobs...
*Googli*[48] snail on the moonlight
*Hele, meteli, dhora, geri*[49] for piles and fischer
They have no shame, no five-fines for stupidity
Continuous parade in their mouths - Hi Dhoni! You
are unique.

4.
Everything is wrong as their *Sargam*[50]
Wrong words, wrong tone of voice, in the ear foam of
faulty wine

Cloudy waves of Clarity on girl friend's chest
Two windy pin-pointed shoes in overflowing bra
There's the face, face grazing, kisses on kiss
It may seem to be a fault a little later

It is better to call heaven as heaven, or may *Dilshan*[51]
The wrong way is the calas umbrella, yet a vagabond
There is no sugarcane juice as called SO
A blow of wrong axe on the long neck after drink
Tax collector's lip kisses the glass of whiskey, ah the
galaxy

5.

Counting the waves half-infixed sandman becomes
bankrupt
The ocean laughs to heart, a bag full of rage
occupying the essence of foam
Mischievous tide runs every now and then
Droplet of moon made a chuckle
Water breaks, water breaks body of whom, only the
sand dunes?

Sandman's ear listen song— humming, whispering
and rattling
To nose comes in particle air rows of aromas the
*Mandas*[52]
In the hills of the body, travelers stood
The eyes do not blink, half-broken nose, the foam
breaking cornea
The tongue blown up into pieces, the rough sand
lover
In waves raping waves breaks roughly into fossils
The corpse of sandman is unmarked, the thirst of
wander walks

6.

Sometimes I become afraid of the ring or the
deliberate command
This soap, which supposed to learn
the rules of melting from the ice chunks,
Chuckles by standing in the row in LIC office and
freeze
The grandson of politics with an open umbrella
becomes a young guitarist
We are afraid of if the whisper of cobra turns out to
be the hood of it
There is pain in the lower-abdomen — water comes
to finish in the body,
I feel cramp in legs due to want of water, digging
water,
pain is now sound in poems
Today is 20th May 2008, today virtually house
arrest—

20th May-2008.

*Translated by Manik Saha.*

## Time -machine

Wire, sides are piles of conversing and listening
pit of water
In between a hanging tail, swinging, dwindling
Camera moves ups and down to control
Movement
Immovable sets in the west or rise in the east
About to leave, finally left on a lighter mode
Moving on the footprints of 'no-origin' *Naad*[53]
sound
Light and slim
Catch, if possible

Dance, dear dance, is it gliding ?
In the hands of that naked doll
if you want to set a 'folk-drum' and its 'dhitang'
sound
offer it a spoon full of keying drink
get it the girls named 'tinni' or 'Tutun'
allow it some time, let her speak loud and say, you
want me to dance?
Arm-pit is hangered and moving as a pendulam
not able to lift its hand and sing the song ' In
my heart...'
another time-cum-myme
it goes on to do it all in sugar and tea
in the key-board's space
in control and shift
it moves and goes for
dumped and haggered
'roulette' dance..
catch, if you can

By not saying 'bye' the 'rein' says to leave
The Deer
At the leap of time's soundscape
It holds a Thermometer instead of hairs in the
arm-pit

Parts of sixty seconds
You may break it more and more and more
These breakages are nothing but pieces of time
Time's rhythmic cold wave in the arm-pit of time
goes for a go
Bip bip bip bip bip bip
Steps to steps musical note, and the band is a rat
At the rat-trap
The rat is dancing laundering and is in no mood to
taste the poison
Sick— fears of ninety degree
Hundred eighty eyes
Are on the run at the beating of time
Mixing the beats with no-beats
Trembled and shaken
As if a war have started between life and death
See, a slip may occur in beating boots or at the happy
looks
Catch, bro catch
You couldn't
Though, the wind is snubbed

ups and down
even in the reverse of that, who is he
Charlie Chaplin, no?
what's up, what's the matter
inflated laugh, moustache, gnat turns to a fearsome
hat?
woops, throat is grasped, eyes are needled
The walking stick is spoilt

In the 'mid-sea' water behaves like a 'co-wife'
Time has come for anchoring
Give rest to those haul and oar
Getting it? Not yet?
Though it seems that it is getable
Or you are still in confusion?
Not able to measure the length, breadth and
perforation?
Is it the slough, kept before the slip?

A Watch can hide innumerable eyes
And shows only three
They pull it for a bath, yields an evening and a lying
pillow
Chicken's crowing sounds on egg-rolls
Minnow bubbles in the fish-egg
In the winter session petrol, sensex, sex,
masturbation roars
Paired trees, swingy kisses, orgasm
Eye stops, no fuel
But it never stops as it doesn't know how to stop
It is not that 'very important' persona
Whom the watch darns to become threads
it goes on to release threads
Till death

That softened warmth beneath slough of this most
complex machine
that L(life) to D(death) encircling game
listening to it's rattling sound
the crematorium plays Kabadi
the 206 decoration of the body
movement of red cells
phlegm and bile at the bondage of bone and flesh at a
local game 'Dariabanda'
Oh, those glozing and nursing

It's an unknown bird
Try to hold it!

Palm holds the myth of a 'godly fish' that saved
civilization
Equal fusion and dissolutions
From those mild pains
Seeds are kept at the 'farm-yard'
Ornaments at lockers
Wind blows and goes on to blow, never leaves the
global truth

Spiral water lays all over the body
Sea unbound
Born to the time's play of game
A start in love
So, players, don't think that there is no starting block
No birth
No 'zero', at the mean of the graph of minus and plus
If you keep, it would go
If it stays, it would not be content
It slips
It is euphoric
Can you hold or touch it?

Tutun, a girl, she is running short of time
Tinni, the other girl and she has a problem with her
Robot
It's not obeying the remote controlled time-span
To measure the time, she has to re-run it
Then a calculation will work
For life
For time
And it can predict the life-span too

If the time gets a re-birth in the 'idiot machine'
Put a conch-shell on the time itself

*Translated by Swapan Roy.*

# Southwest Equinox

## Earns on Beggary — 1 & 5

1
The door open
    The wide open door
The door

The window open
    The window shamelessly open
The window

The open drawer
    The whole of it open
The table

All open
    Unveiled
Everything

Thinking about myself
        I smile mockingly
Cannot actually open up.

5.

Ailing lyrics trespass the sleep
The dreams play raga *Ashabari*[54]
The moonlit autumn and
Blue cast of their domesticity

In the daring of the lonely room shapes of fear
Were there ever any furniture at all?
When the vases sleep
Fragrances of shower beckon dusk

Is there grains of sound from conch shells lying
around?
As if in dance movements the chirps of birds
The unconscious rise
There is an invitation for all to their dance show

For them, one cup of night light is their
Do re mi of the dawn.

## The Leftover Vessel and Shelter

1

The dusts of lost path below the feet
Some places as in *Kishoreganj*[55]
Rivers like *Karnafuli*[56]
And off places
The lines of trees are footsteps along with their music
Keep moving and moving

2

When train windows sleep
Boats from rivers climb up eyes
The bridge and the clatter in cameras wherein dies
the last poetic lines
Thereby *Natore*[57] lies a lesser Banalata
Anchored in earth and spring hearts

8.

Moving on, the vision became eyes
The Reindeers
Selling out nights like *Kumilla*[58] and *Chittagong*[59]
The dawn juggling one yawn with another
As if Manirul will arrive in open, hand in hand with
the creepers of desire

12.

Two eyes behind illusion
Stoop to pick up the scarves
The buds and blossoms overwhelm
The hand fan, even today calls for the mother
The mother calls for the house
You may not find the path to the house
Though restless

## Ma, Opens up the Details

1
The eyes of mine open
   as drops of you
         fall upon me
With those eyes
I see you whole
   in the fragments

2
The hands that put moist closed on fevered head
        Still holds
    The thread from the center
         I revolve.

4
At crematorium
I was anointing the naked alphabets
    The smoke, showed formless poetry

5
Girl
  Dangling
Earrings
   Swaying in probability
      Like mother

10
Not in sleep
     Rather you are looking
Whether the coat button has traced
        the genital passage or not

12.

The pain
  The uterus opening up
Reentering
   Expectancy

14.

A road named Mother
    Not turnings only
       Just broken
Go find out you swine

*All Translated by Debadrita Bose.*

# Dropped Eyes

## Stairs

As I take down my glasses
My eyes drop too
Where do I keep them?

Will this planet jolt out of its orbit? Or was
It out of the track till date
Now the dropped eyes will sit in the orbit
As if a wandering parrot takes recluse on a perch

The resembling birds shredding wing drops from
their beaks
In front of a swing
As a hoopoe calls, I know at least today
Buddies will drop by
The ones who taught me flying with my clinched fists.

I place my eyes on the stairs, they watch the ups and
downs
Watch you going down for the last time
And now, it's me... standing all alone...

## Charcoal

A mad woman sunshine drools down into
The old girl's skin
So crease, so waves inside the hollow mouth
Moonface someday, swallowed stylish moments
The moment I talk about love
It's poetry
The old girl, in this winter sunny afternoon, once
again
Leans to poetry

Carbon flows, poison grunts, bitter wind hides
They all can be joined with a hyphen
Let it be equal let it not be let them enjoy a game of
balances
And sway and dance through this time

No news of any death today… that's the news
No slogans on the walls, that too a statement of its
kind
Only the old girl walks towards the crematorium…
the charcoal...
Hip hip hoorraaaa
Let the evening flowers make a river out of sound…

## Journey

Let all the birds loose out their happy-feathers
In a cacophony season journey
Let them sit on the growing bed of the winter stream
Let the winter skin move towards the summer
And even if it's a bit, let monsoon be
Inside the summer

I keep the wet, I stay wet
I don't keep my lips and heart dry
I don't sing the music of life without even knowing it
The spool isn't moving, the kite is still in the heaven

Burning... attachments, obsessions
Burning ... bones and flesh, and *Om Shaanti*[60]
Bravo Shaanti, one which is scribbled on the
Walls of a crematorium
I know that everything's burning still don't move
away
Let the heat

The smell says about the breath of a different life
Am I that monsoony summer, summery winter!
Or, just a simpleness of that realization...

## Hope

I keep the kids inside the hole of a hole
Inside the hole... hay love inside... picking softness
I'm there the kid of kids... kid of her
Want to be

May be I'd be able to say Adieu
Drinking tea chapbooks
Bagfull of ordered groceries
Out of the brink of a sleep

They would put some hues from a rainbow into my
beak
They would bring some humming tunes from the
filled up pots
Love from the walking eyes behind the curtain of light

As I add the tune to my lovely life, fear's all gone
Wings sway... I fly....
Leaving behind the hopes stored in the hole....

## Beauty Seller

Some pearls off the colours
Un-noticed
Some ducks fly
Suddenly
Peel off skin from the
Words
That lapis lazuli....

Beautiful plants and soap
Strips
Wintery
Falling moonstone
Swims through the prayers
Soft
Fingers
Gathers
Rubykiss bangles...

Dancing lips ting tong
Beauty selling emerald

*All Translated by Kaushik Chakrabarty.*

## Write Poems

When I do hear horse neighs from the byre
Before getting startled I hold myself
Pell-mell are very often now-a-days
Celebrated cricketer conducting show business so
nicely
We all are charmed

The *Shefali*[61] plant of the town should be axed down
Its overgrown branches crossed neighbour's
boundary,
The little Plant likes to bloom crazy but failed due to
water dearth
None are there to watering; those were planted for a
photo-session
The live telecast of that show was a super hit.

If I dangle something to poems, inappropriate for
everyone
You would say ear-ring, an irritating ornament
If I retain myself, I may resembled Great Karna
without Bow and Arrow
When Police arrested me first time with Cannabis
and pipe
To get myself released I murmured, "Write poems"

Whole Police station busted into laughter...

## Jokes and Magic

It's not a matter of joke
Joke is present...

The mosquito-net hanged itself without any hooks
Who, who gets into it! Into a box— like canopy,
negligible as a decimal point
The sleepless night is full of fun, with smiley
stone-face and Magic-stick in hand

Dreams appear, so many unseen dreams
Still eyes are wide open, counting 57, 58, 59....
Holes in mosquito net....
Changing rhythms of its whim, Anopheles tunes
charms of Rabindra-songs
Applying this upon my bed ridden sores
What a comfort, what an ease getting lost into void

Now, hum-hum... trala... tare ...trala.... hum-hum
The magical spirits spreads around mosquito net,
walls, on the ceiling
Musical ornaments drop from the years effortlessly
The sleeping pill forgets the journey from mouth to
stomach
Even the celebrating holy night-lamp refuses to be
glossy

Ample of my dogmas, all of my amenities just made
me a joker
simply a joker, with their entrusted amusement
and gloomy dreams have been waiting and waiting
and waiting
The blob-shaped anopheles has gotten their realms
of languid body

Hypnotized the whole environment

Isn't that a magic? Magic disappears
May I have been a malarial impatience?
Bubbles of garbled words coming out in full swing

It might be a poem or not to a poem
Might be mixed baffling or binary puzzles...!

## Canopy

We may take a little nap beside the narration
Intensity of darkness might be increased if we want
Obstinacy lies beside the sleep, let it be there
Let the rattles be ring, let it ring and dance
Let the *Chhou*[62] masks be oscillate around the room
They are still vigilant, still...

We could measure the quake if Metro ran over your head
The deviation of a hair also makes me tremble
That wide drain which running parallel with your awakening
It handling the spool of glass-dust polished thread to play tricks of Kites
Kites are playing mutual slaughter from its hand with a spool
Trouble saving Baachu lives around somewhere, here or there....

There were no space even for a dot, so demon can be kept
Dissimilarity exists, so someone is either a rose or a Nigerian
Now it is your turn to set the bed besides the analogy
And we might supposedly think your thin bed is your Atlantic
Since long you, thy and myself are lingering on descriptions only.

## Endless Waiting

The throat became dry woods
Sands are unaware, waters dripping from your wet
finger,
Pearl rings are drooping as raindrops
From slow to gradually faster
Is it dream or hallucinations!
Dream may mislead me, you can't

The silver plate is holding all kind dry fruits
These tasteless fruits never paid entrance fees to get
into my lips
Smiling fruit skins tries to please but my keen
expectations
Seems fairy-night under the lamp post

Light was glowing on top of the light house
And muddy water stained the swirling stair case
Your clever feet know the style for descending
At whenever I try, at each step
I myself slip off the stairs.

You Darling, you're last but one line of my poem
My few infant words without helmet....

*All Translated by Umapada Kar.*

# Anarkali's Tanpura

## Earns on Beggary: 11

suppose a meet
    on return to a connection
but no exchange of words first time
suppose a spell of intoxication...
Intensified night is cut into
    two halves by the saw and
circling round two cycle wheels...
    while roaming about  eyes turn on
    the earlier radius of cycle-spokes
and see the left-out days of bathing...
and forelocks reflected on mirror...

already held the smiling stanzas of children's home.
    they too have known the
    tales of moon
    the full-moon's spark...
the facilitating overpasses reduces the
length of routes...
now turning back makes me feel
    the day's dawning blossom.

the return
provides much a differing salt
a taste of crystal as if I come across
  first time...

## Earns on Beggary: 16

the robust snaky darkness swallows
                                        faint shadows
the mirror may now turn to be widow...
the vermilion still looks to be the same.
formulas are very simple and flexible.

the east plays with purple glow youth of
        east and the mirror
        putting off its own tiara
decorates its reflected forehead.
the shadow-born darkness yields
                        song-prone elation...
the mirror turning blushed rouses the
                        imagery of pomegranate
on the dead lipsticks.

whether the shadow runs after darkness
        or darkness after the shadow is unknown to the
                                                        mirror.
far beyond the east on west 's cape
the evening candles' singing-anklets
not again known to the mirror.
it only holds tight on its breast
thousands of suddenness
      some lemons and some of its juice...

## Earns on Beggary: 21

tea liquor is getting mixed
with current affairs.
lots of knick-knack perceptions brimmed
        on the mythical round-table
        linking to the earlier clues...
        some ranks of desired-kins on the
length of a cubic day are cleansing off
in the softness of extensive tract.
a bird of prey constantly soaring up
unending height and
descending as soft water-lilies...

a protruded part of building, a balcony
where lies upside down the omnibus
                                        on easy chair
spread out thereby some medicines
                                    and perfumes...
another round of tea is served with an
affectionate maternal hand
          dangling the end of *Sari*...
some left-out threads received
from a kite got cut while flying...
some relations with whom
    furnished the platters and the relations
    can one after another be easily flown now...

## Earns on Beggary: 24

it does'nt matter, you said,
        don't know why.
showed the cleavages and folded them
with covers.
the sun couldn't peep out.
        doesn't it matter ?

does ever Spring come if a caterpillar
is blended with a gallop-run?
no, never, the Spring approaches that way.
        never it does...
searching eyes may find some cut-out
pine apples... may find even some sweat
and itchy skins.
        doesn't it matter
a chameleon from the nave hangs ?

scattered your hair
on what doesn't occur.
dropped a mass of darkness at the entrance
        to the underworld...
standing with lips wide open at its front door
calls me at the eaves of your back door,
as if I'm to slip down to it in monsoon
        doesn't it matter, say, doesn't it!

## Earns on Beggary: 30

shirts are enjoying the *Shravana*[63]
on several hangers
the chest-ribs bursting in the
    thunderous sky.
    so-much water elsewhere
yet the day's thirst is to satisfy only with
watermelons...
a seller with *Makhan*[64] -balm couldn't go down on
    vending the items today...

the fetters will hardly last long to tie the intangible
    dark-lings.
tied with other fetters as much as
    multiplications and divisions.
knowing this all procures may slip off
anytime, the corpse of heavy shakles
is sitting with all plus and minus...

the fetters can't entangle me
rather I'm entangling them...

## Earns on Beggary: 39

quietude would get wet if didn't
stand aside unseen.
the armpit won't catch hold of it
and prior to someone's understanding
        of anything
behind naked camouflage
resonance meter gets intensified...

the quietude here acts as coins
        In the dead-man's pocket.
it is flying anywhere else
insisting on us to wait for head and tail
      tossing, but not coming down
on our palm nor on grass.
i wonder if the tail-mark is suggested
        on both sides of the coin.

fire, fire is found everywhere
        holding in its grip
        the notch of blowing wind
there rests no light at all, darkness too nowhere
                                                    found.
        no warmth, so the frozen
but wise baloon can hardly fly.

fire likes to suffer in burns unseen
fire likes to set fire on stony heart
and perennial tales of motionlessness...

*All Translated by Alok Biswas.*

## Untitled -1

Laid, at ease
  Didn't keep the click

Denied me too
  Why to keep the snap!

## Untitled -2

Going back to
    Hypotenuse

Yet to forget
   Circle's setting out

Standing on base
    Resting on perpendicular

Not able to back again
    Circle makes me a circumference...
       Spinning is unbearable

## Untitled -9

A look from innerself
Ruled striped
Flyovers...

Comes down
Takes a flight
Leaving a mom like shadow...

I move I roam I take a spinning dive
Coming down
Stopping
Beside 'this way's sideway...

Everyone cross pass me, shadow like
Me only left with a land of immobility...

## Untitled - 10

Wished not
   Never ever wished
Yet you refused

Kept both ways
  A large cosmos
Illusionary

Showing a way to the light
   Before the path ends

Sleep appears
   I return it to my fingers
 In terror
 In sense
Sleep never comes to the doorstep...

## Untitled - 13

I made you to listen
The falling sound of pain
And me too listened it

Heavy winds
Not able to make a way out
Looks helplessly at the mirror

In the reflection it seems like pain-camphor on a drop of water
Ray says, light...
To be a light

I am running for that
You too join me...

## Untitled - 15

Violin reads
  Pained household
  In a book of grammar

Pages of multiplication table
  Chewed by the belch-inclined cannon

Confounded me
   Not knowing my 'do's and 'don'ts
     Salute the cow
   And down my head to its toe

The flute gently
   Picks off its lips from the embouchure hole
   In a moment

## Untitled - 18

Your rejoicing is in the sky, balcony in the air
The crow of spring hangs as 'Come-September'

As if a calendar
Partly blown in your hair-do
Like the solitary morning mist
Calling irritatingly and excessively
The touring stupid crow...

Firebrand grapes
Decanter overflowed with caw caw
The sour winter fruit *aamlaki*[65] exceeds the melting
point in cuckoo's note
It awakens the squeezed snake from hibernation

Lip clad look is on the foot-finger's nail
Gossip whispers with a sense of disbelief in the
blowing air
Never you allowed me to touch your shadow and
humble load of breast
Taken aback the endangered crow is now trying
to be a cuckoo
A cannonball of fear grasping its voice
Clavicle holds that mark of fear
Afterglow of spring

*All Translated by Swapan Roy.*

# Untitled Dolls

## Doll - 1

A doll in the picture is absorbed, juggling sun in one
hand
It bears girlish features
Could be delicate as well
As it has not burnt the palms

After waiting for a while, it starts to skip
Finally hanging the ball,
In the void of a twilight circus

The girl on the opposite,
Seems to be prepared too...

## Doll - 2

A spring-wind-up doll
Has been seated before a graph sheet
The doll plays a drum automatically with the winds

Each square of the graph sheet
Is overflowing with atoms of sound
When the music stops
A violin could be spotted behind
But the bow is missing
As the sketch remained incomplete
For want of winds in the spring

## Doll - 3

An old time doll, when taken out of the cupboard
Shies away from his battery-operated modern peer
For being too sheepish or stupefied
And, wonders at the situation

It reminds him of a similar old world doll, some forty
years back
And her reluctance to bond with him
Since she was a lady

Now, would he muster enough courage
To approach the latest bobbed and skimpily-clad
doll?
Would he touch her fingers... or the glowing radiance
of skin?

## Doll - 9

None of the dolls arrived, despite repeated
assurances
So did the monsoon
None of the dolls departed
Even with numerous affirmations
The spring has bid farewell

Puppet-crazies have met in a rendezvous somewhere
In the reflected lunar halo
It will rain, today or tomorrow
The lunatics will chill out
Although their insanity would fill up
The nursery bed of paddy seeds
And a gentle breeze will glide softly
Over their cheeks

## Doll -12

When the pillars are overcast with thick clouds
'Deep' rests in the cast of a doll
Revived by rains,
It would laugh, romp and wave at friends in the
school bus

It would simply lick the ecstasy-in-residue
And life trickles down, into corpse
The mortals, who never thought about rejuvenation
With a life— virtually from birth

## Doll - 15

I wanted to decorate the dolls by illuminating them
I observed they brim with zeal thereafter
And cascade upon the carpet from cupboard
With overflowing joy

I am ignorant about the rules of their game
Yet I play and lose frequently
Barring for a doll which loses to me consciously and giggles
Glancing at my pitiable face
If I manifest any sign of gratitude
It breaks into laughter
I lie down with this one
While placing the others back in cupboard
Then we laugh together in bed
And the chuckle embraces all our triumphs and failures

## Doll - 24

Some dolls are barely dolls
Some are substantial
Yet others remain in transition
All are disgruntled about their position
They tease among themselves and jeer at each other
Which are no pleasure bickering
But a conscious effort to pull down one another
By malicious strategies
And fling low

When the dolls collectively achieve to knock down
any of them
They trample over
And on top of these,
A bruised doll's diary-writing terminates forever

*All Translated by Bhaswati Goswami.*

## Untitled – Two

Today the fifth day of nonstop raining
A day free of any name as Sun Mon Tuesday
The Fifth is its identity
Inviting them all I show its blackish face
and the temperate air
Only air makes disheveled all, even to the interior
Who are you being nostalgic sing a song in this air?
drink repentance
Who are you catch hold in palms the disordered air
collecting the news of depression?
Who are you, an irritated one for want of a special
day name?
Go once ups and down to make you wet with the
air
Advance towards east and then to south
Tell me, whether you are now free from burden or not
So that one can mix oneself up with the air
on the fifth day same as reduced burden

## Untitled – Nine

It needs bow-down to the feet of oneself everyday
With own effort, a little
Someone knows it, feels it
And measuring the shadow one keeps it inside a journal
Someone supercilious bothers not
They don't bow-down nor measure the inclination

A period persists that comes within six seasons
Somebody observes the combination, 'A' with 'A' or 'E'
Only a little part of muslin slimy
At some places it tallies possibly, somewhere it doesn't
Only dissatisfaction and the mind becomes inexplicable
Someone else doesn't care at all for that comparison
They know it well that conciliation is impossible
Then why for nothing a journey to the void journal
putting on the spectacle

Bowing down everyday I wish to get sunshine in the afternoon,
may it be setting down

## A Child of Light and Darkness

Mixing shadow with light this is Derjeeling and
Dooars
A day with tea color
will be presented to me
uttered so long ago
Not you, your enthusiastic nature will offer this
But what shall I do with this presentation!
If the child continues to cry and the whining rain
wants to suppress the mouth of the child again and
again
Is it any indicator for the conversion of the lighted
day to darkness?
For which no meter has yet been invented to
measure
What shall I do with this light mixed with shadow?
How can I satisfy my taste of tea, if the child of
Derjeeling
doesn't play together with the child of Dooars!
If one makes face with another and the other
doesn't burst out with laughter!

*All Translated by Umapada Kar.*

# Uncollected Poems

## Untitled -1

I turn all the names drifted to me into conveyance.
Someone is bi-cycle while someone sailing boat.
I make someone a missile
so that it can hit the target rightly.

Playing with fire, and my cruel game is behind
that very missing flight.
It's my curved finger by which that launch is
oscillating vigorously
and the passengers are shouting for help.

This grotesque game wants to wake all from slumber.
All its desire and intention is encircling the robot.
The folded palm intends to get the love and affection
of the machine-man for its own.

'Alas' is the appropriate word here
in place of that I write another name of a vehicle,
not invented yet
but still exists in one's notion.

07/09/2017

## Untiled - 2

The words of intense affliction may rest aside
keep apart the erased afternoon whisperings.
Please come to share thc fresh pleasure of the morning,
Just now, before the sun becomes thickened reddish.

Sleeping bedstead has not kept words, nor the pillow too.
Still I am fresh after a sleepless night.
This is with an anticipation to complete my bath
with a little jocund-water.

Report of your sleep may be beyond my knowledge.
I don't know, how much dense were the curtains
of windows
to prevent light from outside,
or how much influenced you were
being wrapped by the zeal of quilt.
Looking you fresh also, that's enough.

Who are those to mix the sound of morning flute with
air?
Let's think that is for ours,
friends with sugarless tea hope that we shall be
glad,
sloth air holds the sugar-pot in hand, if it needs a
little.

The morning is waiting only for us from the dawn.
Please come, let's enter, and exchange our places.
Let's share the amassed melancholy
which is part of pleasure as bonded by wedding.

13/09/2017

## Untitled - 3

Chameleon pulls its hand back after touching lightly.
Warp of *sari* is in metamorphoses colour,
weaving out flying butterfly,
nothing can be better than this.

Windows of the closed room are opened after a long
period,
but sunshine is scarce today.
Dampish, few moist frog's croaking are entering
the room.
This is also a special gift like rainbow.

Some kites are flying in the sky at their heart's
content,
the horizon is giving cordial reception to their
behavior like whirling, curved dipping, and
ups and down.
Globe is rounding on its own imagined spine aside,
and within this periphery we the small
perpendiculars stand erect.

Anxiety is noticed in all, useless laugh,
only butterflies and kites are flying away on *saris*
and in the sky.
These are allotment for us to release the skin of
concern.

19/09/2017

## Untitled - 4

The accumulated words in a series of crease are
almost torn,
bringing out from the breast-pocket
they tear once again more a little.
Ah! The words behind words get pains more,
and few drops of blood become confused instead
of congelation.

Many persons save up antique and ancient.
They bring down them off and on.
New dress is necessary after the job,
some new devices are also the need to be inspired
with new hope.
Nothing can be done if it seems a dream.

Once again they are to be stored after setting in order
as previous
as a part of a game.
Existence of traditional shape and routine is absent,
still a craze persists,
and so many drafts work for exempting the craziness.
Ah! Don't startle with amazement
if the words come spontaneously 'God forbid'
at the time of rearranging them.

08/10/2017

## Untitled - 5

The mind becomes delighted by few drops of aroma.
I am scattering myself the whole day and night.
Flash of delight on the face of public.
Bowing their heads the mob is passing away
calling me an extraordinary constantly.

I don't know anything about this
I was walking simply in the middle of them,
even not laughing, a fright made me puppet from
the beginning.
Then, why all of them are so pleased
and why they bend their heads from shoulders.

All they are reading me thoroughly, targeted me
minutely.
And they have seen certainly such a thing within
me
so that I have no alternative but to startled.
I am enjoying this utmost, though sweating internally.

10/10/2017

## Untitled - 6

Non-existent, still the 2 BHK flat seems to be there

Two floating buoys inside, still I think, they aren't
Yet drifting, with what a magic?

I am inside the room, obsessed, the two rooms seem
to be limitless
It seems a little opening will never end

Mortgaged to my wrapper
paying the interest without caring for the principal

The lizard on the wall with astonishment
search of insect-shadow in the deep sunshine
in the midst of have and have-not

Even the hand, throwing stones at the incomplete
honeycomb,
all that remains, stays.... assuring my departure

15/10/2017

## Untitled - 7

The glory of journey tries to loosen the interlockings
Moves and spreads out
Though, they don't relax by any means

The pains are kept into the bell-jar of joy
Hoping that they get the pleasure-touch
Tries to bloom as happiness but fails

Who gets selected by a concept named life while
trying to be astonished
Where involvement is the obvious
And simply crotons of suffering

Here joy is the camphor, colorful gas-balloon of
religion swells more
where lives the primordial man
those who are every now and then mortal

Chariot drawn by seven horses fly in the hands of kids
They promise to take us, unwinding
Opening the faces of pain

16/10/17

**Untitled - 8**

I come back time and again to this malicious bedstead
How much scandalous it is in domestic life
Stupidity for demand of infatuation

The room beside is fully vacant, without any furniture
Still the legs are yet to back there
As if the bed and pillows are smeared with glue

Failing to be one's own I get afraid in the vacant
Void is not always a void, rather some more
condensed emptiness.
Is then this lively face of air glum and magically
grave too!

The wind is the only provision in this flight with one
filled and one vacant heart
If it becomes enthusiastic for murdering or
becomes more illiberal
It forgets to give a little puff to my toy flute

I shall have to come back to the bedstead dumping
the fluttering into the garbage

I want it or not the bedstead is my shelter,
My main goal is to make it giggle with any flattery
If a little separation can make it joyful

20/10/2017

**Untitled - 9**

I intend to establish my foothold
In the space more soothing than salt
One kind of comfort is there in fire
Which our boyhood knew well at the event of
burning chick-peas
It's only panic today and gist of crematorium

White pigeon is an amazing relax
for the gem of eyes and the blue sky
I need it forever, even in between workouts
Often I get it beyond the reach, in the light of
darkness for a moment
like the few disappearing dots in the black fume air.

For drifting I will not get back that banana raft
Let then the prayer for the wheel continue
I need the assurance which is rare and hangs in the
opposite
Umbrella hides only the sunshine upon whatever
is of mine
I haven't desired this shadow while moving,
But still then

25/10/2017

**Untitled - 10**

Listen, this discharge from the gall-bladder is not
mine
It's meaningless to be a clown in the family of
guinea-pigs
Still, why do I keep all the homeopathy vials neatly
on the shelf...
They also laugh out being tickled, my hands are so
soft and they are so sensitive

You put the crown of thorn on to the childhood which
loves lozenges, at the littlest of chance
You need to think... how much blood stain does the
cockle full of milk get?
Everyone rears snakes, only an exorcist is identified
He knows how to play the kettledrum, others do not

Afternoons designed with signs have arranged
cosmetics for me
It seems... enough... enough.... Let me make myself up
The clown market high now
Let the Thousands of customers look also at me at
least once

Turning into a commodity I completely forget about
the discharge from the gall-bladder
Forget the vials of medicine, and a snake plays on its
tail
Inside me

25/10/2017

*All Translated by Umapada Kar.*

## End Notes

1. Chhoto Nagpur – A hiily area of Jharkhand, India.
2. Gazan – The festival of lord Shiva.
3. Chaitra – The last month of the year in Bengali calander. Part of Spring .
4. Kubo bird – A brownish colour bird looks like crow.
5. Ghat – Landing stages at pond river etc.
6. Sundarban – A Mangrove area along with 'Sundari', 'Genoa', 'Garan' trees at the coast of Bay of Bengal.
7. Farakka – A big barrage cum bridge in West-Bengal over river Ganga.
8. Kalahandi – A place of Orrisa, India, The name associated with backwardness, famine, and starvation death.
9. Rohini – Name of a star in Bengali.
10. Kishoreganj – A place of Bangladesh.
11. Gayan Gosai – A prominent music director of undivided Bengal.
12. Bibhuti – Full name, Bibhutibhusan Bandopadhyay. An important Novelist of Bengali literature of India.
13. Illyas – Full name, Akhtaruzzaman Illyas. An important Novelist of Bengali literature of Bangladesh.
14. Bishad Sindhu – Sea of sorrow. A Novel in Bengali written by Mir Musharaf Hossain.
15. Madari ka khel – (A phrase in Hindi) A special type of play with magic, jugglery, illusion etc shown by the wandering tribes. This is their source of earning.
16. Khoai – Cobbled streets at Shantiniketan, A university founded by Rabindranath Tagore.
17. Madari – Same as 15.
18. Anna – Currency unit formerly used in British India.
19. Shivgazan – The festival of worshipping Shiva.
20. Sherwani – A special type of dress of Indian male.
21. Ulupi – A beautiful lady dancer of heaven as per Hindu

Puran.

22. Tekka – Superior Playing Card.
23. Saheb – King Playing card, next to Tekka.
24. Bibi – Queen Playing card, next to King.
25. Ardhakurmasana – One type of posture of Yogic exercise.
26. Falguna – Name of a month in Bengali calandar. Part of spring in Bengal.
27. Palasha – A special type of flower in the eastern part of India.
28. Kharisa – One type of snake with severe venom.
29. Rohotang – A pass in high altitude at Himalaya (Himachal Pradesh, India).
30. Poush-Pitha – Various types of sweet cake made of Rice-powder prepared in the last day of the month 'Poush'.
31. Ishti Kutum – One type of yellow-black coloured bird in Bengal.
32. Kutum – Relatives esp. allied by matrimony.
33. Jamrul – One type of all most tasteless fruit of Bengal.
34. Dopatta – One kind of dress of ladies in Northern India.
35. Cheli – Same as above.
36. Alvida – An word in Urdu language. Means, to see one off (Goodbye).
37. Dalma – A mountainous forest at Jharkhand, India.
38. Bhangra – A special type of folk dance of Punjab, India.
39. Ghat – Same as endnote no 5.
40. Rai – Young Radhika, beloved of Lord Krishna.
41. Mahua – Local made wine from Mahua fruits.
42. Kirtan – Any of the songs about Radha and Krishna.
43. Nagkeshar – A beautiful flower of Bengal.
44. Nataraj – A special type of gesture of dancing of Lord Shiva.
45. Matrabritta – One type of Bengali meter out of three meters of Bengali Verse.
46. Yajna – Vedic sacrifice or offering in fire.
47. Malkosh – An Indian musical Raga.

48. Googli – Aqatic living being, generally born in pond, river etc.

49. Hele, meteli, dhora, geri – Types of different venomless snakes.

50. Sargam – Indian musical octave.

51. DilShan – An word in Urdu language. Means, cheerful.

52. Mandas – One type of floating arrangement, mainly made of Banana tree and Bamboo.

53. Naad – Sound which comes out from the navel of human being.

54. Ashabari – One type of Indian musical mode (Indian Classical Raga).

55. Kishoreganj – Same as end note no 10.

56. Karnafuli – A river of Bangladesh.

57. Natore – A small town of Bangladesh.

58. Kumilla – A big town of Bangladesh.

59. Chittagong – Officially Chattogram. 2nd Largest City of Bangladesh at the coast of Bay of Bengal.

60. Om Shaanti – The mystic sound referred in Hinduism, the origin or root of all sounds, spreads peace and calm.

61. Shefali – A type of small white flower of Bengal blossoms in Autum.

62. Chhou – A folk dance form of Bengal with different types of masks.

63. Shrabana – Name of a month of Bengali Calendar. Mainly Rainy season.

64. Makhan – Name of a balm product.

65. Aamlaki – One type of fruit, sour in taste.

## Acknowledgement

It is the space where I can express my gratitude to all, associated with this collection. First of all, I pay my heartiest love to all the translators of the collection. They are my friends, and some of them are my younger poets. With their busy schedule, they have done the job with love and joy within the time frame. Acknowledging them through my expression of gratitude will be a little. In this moment of thinking, I want to give all of them a big hug as a symbol of my love and affection for the younger ones. I shall give special thanks to Runa Bandyopadhyay, who is attached from the beginning of the project with her proper suggestions. I would also mention Alok Biswas and Kaushik Chakrabarty for their assistance in other fields. I am grateful to Rohon Kuddus, the publisher of the collection, a writer also, who has taken all positive steps to make this collection a good one. I am also grateful to Debashish Saha, an eminent artist, who has created the cover of this book. Last but not least, I am obliged to my senior poet Murat Nemat-Nejat, who agreed to write the preface of the book. Expression of any type of gratitude is not sufficient for him. I may only say 'be well sir'.

With Regards and Love

**Umapada Kar**

## Introduction of the Poet

Umapada Kar is an important Bengali poet and essayist of contemporary Bengali New poetry. His magnificent and multidimensional poems objectify an object to refer to its properties with a centrifugal journey by decentralizing consciousness. His poems create an imaginary space with the refracted light of his own experiences and are aversive to any conventional poetry institute. He was born and brought up in Beharampur, Murshidabad in 1955 and presently lives in Kolkata, India. He has done graduation in physics and was working in a Nationalized Bank. He was co-editor of 'Shrabosti' and associated with 'Rourob' little magazine. He was associated for a few years with performing art like drama, theatre, recitation, symbolic drama, dance drama, etc. He was also participating in debates, seminars, speeches, etc. His first poetry book Rituporber Nach (Dance of Seasonality) published by Kobita Pakhshik in 1996 (Writing period: 1979 - 1987). After that, he authored several poetry books: Koyek Alokborsho Dure (Few Light-years Away, pub: Roktomangso, 2002), Porijayee Cholo (Move on Migration, pub: Rourob, 2005), Bhanga Piyanor Paa (Leg of Broken Piano, Pub: Bhashabondhan, 2009), Apor Bosonta (The Other Spring, Pub: Kobita Campus, 2009), Dhonuk Kothay Swar (Vowels to Bow Words, Pub: 9ya Doshok, 2011),

Nodite Sayong Bhese Jay (Floating Twilight of River, Pub: Ekhon Bangla Kobitar Kagoj, 2014), Aalor Hnasuya (Light of Scythe, Pub: Kaurab, 2016), Noirite Bishube (In the Southwest Equinox, Pub: Akash, 2017), Namiye Rakha Chokh (Dropped Eyes, Pub: Srishtisukh, 2018), Aanarkolir Tanpura (Anarkali's Tanpura, Pub: Ekhon Bangla Kobitar Kagoj, 2019), Shironaamheen Putul (Untitled Dolls, Pub: Tristup, 2019). Collection of long poems Balumanusher Jhunjhunat (Jingling of Sandman, Pub: Sristisukh, 2016). He also authored prose books: Riledourer Anishesh (The Endless Relay Race, Pub: Aihik, 2017), Rabindra Kobita: Ajker Uthone (Poetry of Rabindranath: In Present Day, Pub: Khorimati, 2017), Aabahaman Path: Tero Aakash (Traditional Reading: Thirteen Skies, Pub: Sristisukh, 2020). He is a hard-core traveller, loves theatre and songs, and loves Bengali's favourite *adda*. He believes that his poetry world gives him support in all his losses and traumas.

## Introduction of the Translators

**Swapan Roy** (b 1956) is one of the most innovative Bengali writers of the 1980s. He is basically a Rourkelite (Steel city Rourkela). He is focussing on alternative literary pursuits and experiments to open up new spaces for poetry with the sound-play of words. With the introduction of 'New Poetry', an exploration of poetry and poetics in the early 90s, he became one of the pioneers of this exploration. His first poetry book Ami Aschi (The Arrival) published in 1984. And then published Che, Lenin Nagari, Kuasha Cabin, Dure Common Room, Meghantara, Deshraag, Cinema Cinema, etc one by one. He writes also prose regarding poetry. Books are Eksho Surje & Kunchbahar. He is also a frequent translator. He translates mainly into Bengali from other languages. Currently, he is associated with an 'Avant-garde' Bengali magazine on poetry and poetics called 'Natun Kabita' (New poetry).

**Alok Biswas**, one of the representative Bengali poets of the Eighties, editor of the Bengali literary periodical of New Poetry Movement, Kabita Campus since 1991, was born of a lower-middle-class family on 4th November 1959 in the congested small-scale industrial city of Howrah in West Bengal, India. Passing from Calcutta University with English as a special subject, he involved himself in leftist political activities that rendered him the intimate experience of the people living in different strata. His first collection of poetry A Red Horse in the Blue Mirror was published in 1989. To date, he published fifteen collections of poetry including some compilations of poetry and short stories edited by him. Among his notable poetry collections are Makorsar Jaal (cobweb), Virus Balletroom, Shrirupini Dotcom, Rupsa Piano, Atanur Naamgondho, etc. He published a short story collection titled Durovaash Colony in 1997. The compilations of the poetry of the poets of the Seventies, Eighties, and Nineties edited by him are highly acclaimed in India and Bangladesh.

**Aryanil Mukherjee** (b 1964) is a bilingual poet, essayist, translator, and editor who grew up in Kolkata, India, and later emigrated to the United States. He has authored fifteen books of poetry and essays in two languages. Aryanil has translated scores of international poets on both hemispheres including a book-length translation project on John Ashbery. He lives in Cincinnati and works as an engineering mathematician.

**Runa Bandyopadhyay** is a bilingual poet, essayist, and translator in the New Poetry world. Though she is a scientist by profession, yet fully addicted to the drug of innovative experimental literature. In her innovative 'recurring poetry' stream she authored Nocturnal Whistle, in English, published by Cyberwit in 2019, and Antarbarty Pangkti (Between the Lines) and Tamaser Alokbhromon (Light-Travel of the Dark) in Bengali, published by Kaurab in the year of 2012 and 2017 respectively. She transcreated and co-edited the anthology Bridgeable Lines: An Anthology of Borderless World Poetry in Bengali with 12 contemporary American poets in 2019. Apart from that, she authored four Poetry books, two Storybooks, and two prose books in Bengali. She co-edited an anthology Hardcore Kaurab-2 with poet Barin Ghosal, published by Kaurab in 2013. Runa has translated numerous international poets bidirectional between English and Bengali including Charles Bernstein, Murat Nemet-Nejat, Peter Gizzi, Eileen Tabios, Barin Ghosal, Swadesh Sen, Alok Sarkar, etc. She is a regular contributor of poems, and essays in various literary journals, both in print and electronic media. Her poems have been included at The End of the World Project Anthology. She is the Contributing Editor for the magazine Dispatches from the Poetry War.

**Kaushik Chakrabarty** is a poet, essayist, translator, fiction writer, painter & musician. Born on 1st May, 1977, he lives in Kolkata. To date he has published 4 collections of poems: Mayer Lekha Rannaghar (Kitchen as Written by My Mother), 2000; Antarbarti Rupkathar Prachchad (Cover Page of an Interim Fairytale), 2003; Corrugated Overdose, 2007 & Bhasha Haranor Andho Math (The Blind Meadows of Lost Languages), 2011. A regular contributor of poems, essays, short stories, and a novel in leading literary journals, both in print and electronic media, his poems have been included in many well-acclaimed Anthologies. His poems have also been translated into English, Hindi, Kannada & Spanish. He is the recipient of the 'Kabita Pakshik Samman' in 2001 and "Kaalkatha Samman" in 2019. Currently, he is working on the manuscript of his third fiction.

**Bhaswati Goswami**, a resident of Delhi for the last 25 years, was born and brought up in Kolkata. She started learning dance and theatre in 'Children's Little Theatre' from the tender age of 5. In C.L.T she received rigorous training in various forms of classical and folk dances for 12 years under the tutelage of eminent gurus. After settling in Delhi, Bhaswati joined the Bengali News Section of Zee TV. Later she worked in a school for 17 years. At present she acts in a Group theatre, performing all over India and in Dhaka. She also anchors prestigious Government and Non-Government stage programmes in Delhi. Her writing skill spanned over the last ten years. In 2012 she came close to the upholders of Natun Kabita and blossomed as a poet. From the very inception, her metaphors were distinct and different from the others and she left a voice of her own. At the 2015 Kolkata Book Fair, her first book containing a collection of poems with self-translations was published by Natun Kabita Prokashani. The name of the bilingual book on a single cover was 'Bhabna College/ Moon In The Block' for the Bengali and English sections respectively. In the same year, Deep Prokashani published her translated non-fiction 24 Akbar Road originally written by Rasheed Kidwai. Bhaswati keeps herself engrossed in her creative pursuits

**Manik Saha** was born in 1983 and brought up in Dinhata of Coochbehar district. Completed MA in English from BU. Started writing poetry in his early teens when at school and continues to write till now. Translated many poems of various poets for various magazines. The first full-length translated work is Vintage Courtyard originally written in Bengali by Subir Sarkar. Poetry Collections are Chaya Roder Braille, Joljotsnar Meye, and Ashwamedher Ghora— all in Bengali.

**Nilima Deb** was born and brought up in North Tripura. Now, settled in Chennai with her family. Graduated in Science and post-graduated with MBA. Working as a teacher for a CBSC school. She is a prosperous young bilingual Poet in the Bengali and English languages. As a mother tongue, her first priority is Bengali. Her debut poetry book (in Bengali) is going to be published soon. She is also an efficacious bilingual translator. Loves to translate or transcreate poetry from Bengali to English and reverse. She feels that through poetry she can try to value the independence of soul and mind which is the brightest touch that never hurts.

**Debadrita Bose**, born and brought up in Kolkata, is an eminent young poet. She has a degree in English Literature and Language and translation from the University of Calcutta and Jadavpur University, Center for translation of Indian Literature respectively. She is engaged in teaching activities as a profession. Her first book of poetry 'Biral Gandho Theke' (From rare smell) was published in 2014. And the next book's name is Chhaya Piari. She is an associate editor of the Bengali little magazine 'Ashtray' and coordinator at the multilingual online journal 'Indiaree'. She is also a contributor to various academic and literary journals and magazines. Recently she is interested and involved in films. Directed a few short films and was awarded also.

www.ingramcontent.com/pod-product-compliance
Lightning Source LLC
Chambersburg PA
CBHW062136160726
48282CB00027B/840
* 9 7 8 9 3 8 9 9 5 3 4 3 5 *